GREATER T  :

An Inspiring Story of Anxiety Disord_
Recovery and the Creation of a
Global Mental Health Community

BY DEAN STOTT

Cover design: Sooraj Mathew

Edited by Hilary Jastram, www.jhilcreative.com

TESTIMONIALS FROM THE DLC ANXIETY COMMUNITY

The DLC Anxiety community is full of lovely humans and kind souls. As the community has grown, I've been blessed with so much amazing and positive feedback about the work we're doing together.

I want to take a moment to share some of it with you. The power of community in recovery is real.

'Can I just say I love your page so much! Every time I scroll through I feel like I'm in a place where people actually understand me. Thank you!'

'I love how your account shines a light on anxiety, how it can affect people, and that we need to support one another.'

'Thanks for the work that you're doing, especially for males that aren't used to seeing themselves represented in these conversations.'

'Honestly for years I have felt alone and like no one fully understands what is going on in my head. Then I came across this page. And I knew I just had to follow. This page has helped me so much over the last few months when my anxiety attacks have been through the roof. Thank you again!'

'I really enjoy what you're doing with your platform. It's inspiring and uplifting.'

'It honestly means the world to me to know that someone posts and genuinely cares about people with anxiety.'

'Thank you for the great work you are doing to advocate for people like myself who suffer from anxiety.'

'One of my highlights of the year was finding your account. I've learnt so much about what I'm going through and feel less alone. Thank you for all that you do.'

GET INVOLVED!

Get involved with the Greater Than Panic discussion.

Be sure to share your wins, big and small, on your stories, tagging @dlcanxiety and using the hashtag #greaterthanpanic. We love to celebrate and share all your wins! Wins come in all shapes and sizes. It could be getting out of bed, going to the supermarket, or making it through a day at work!

You might face a specific fear or phobia, sit with an anxious response, or find a new tool for your recovery toolkit. No matter what it is, we want to hear about it.

If you haven't already, please join the DLC Anxiety Instagram community:

Become a member of our Facebook group:

Visit our website: www.dlcanxiety.com

If you've enjoyed *Greater Than Panic* or found it helpful in some way, consider leaving a review on Amazon. That would mean the world to us!

TABLE OF CONTENTS

FOREWORD

I was fortunate enough to meet Dean when I was at my lowest mental health state. His DLC Anxiety platform, the community, content, and top-tier Instagram Lives (including my favourite episode with Alessia Cara) helped me recognise that I was not alone. I am honoured to have been a guest of his and to now call him a friend. Thank you, Dean, for providing help to millions around the globe and for breaking the barrier/stigma surrounding mental health.

Greater Than Panic is Dean's real-life experience with grief after the passing of his dad. The grief led to the panic attacks he would battle with every day. Dean takes you to the darkest point in his life, his hardest and most fearful times where he felt trapped, isolated, and hopeless, and shows you how he started to turn the odds in his favour by an innate willingness to survive, motivate, support, and guide. This is a truly inspiring story of mental health success. I believe it will inspire people going through anxiety disorders and others wanting to support those around them who may be struggling. Not only will people find much hope in Dean's book, but they will also be inspired by how he used that painful experience to dedicate his life to giving back to the mental health community. He has created an incredible anxiety-support platform that reaches across the globe, giving people the tools and confidence they need to continue moving forward.

Dean's platform works because he has provided a community for real people to share real stories of anxiety success and struggles. In the DLC Anxiety community, people feel connected, not alone in tackling anxiety, and can learn so much from the incredible interviews Dean provides and the abundance of knowledge and education.

Enjoy the book and be well,

Zach Dereniowski

@mdmotivator

INTRODUCTION

Greater Than Panic **is a book about fear.**

Real fear.
Intense fear.
Crippling fear.

But ultimately, baseless fear, and how I unmasked and moved beyond it.

I hope that *Greater Than Panic* is a book that helps you do this too.

My journey through an anxiety disorder started with some of the scariest moments of my life in 2016 and ended with my full recovery and the birth and growth of the DLC Anxiety online mental health community in 2018.

I wrote this book for anyone struggling with high anxiety, recurring panic attacks, scary intrusive thoughts, agoraphobia, or any of the myriad of common anxiety disorders that impact so many people worldwide every year.

Greater Than Panic is the story of a life taken away by anxiety, then slowly reclaimed. It is a book about hope, never giving up, steering your own ship, and the importance of community and support while you travel the path towards anxiety recovery.

In telling an anxiety story, a recovery story, and the story of how DLC Anxiety became what it is, it is my hope that I will inspire you to take steps towards your own recovery and all that is possible in life. I was lifted up and supported by the experiences and stories of others, so now it is my turn to do the same for those travelling the path I travelled.

It is my sincere hope that you find this book helpful in some way, and I thank you for your love and support.

It means the world to me.

Dean Stott
March 2022

CHAPTER 1

LET IT BEGIN

Suddenly, something was very wrong with me.

Nothing was real.

Everything became peculiar and foreign to me.

My heart was pounding as if I was trying to outrun death.

I could feel myself sweating for no obvious reason, even though I was standing still.

The lights were bright.

Too bright.

Unnaturally bright.

My breathing changed.

I was suffocating.

This was not right.

I was instantly afraid.

All around me, shoppers had stopped and stood, staring intently at me. At least, that's what it felt like. They knew I was in trouble. They knew something was wrong with me. I was sure of it.

My fear grew. A horrible sense of danger and doom encircled me. The belief that something terrible was happening to me burned hotter and hotter with each passing second.

I stopped dead in my tracks, unable to complete the simple task of purchasing milk. The dairy aisle of my local supermarket had instantly transformed into a twisted, unreal, distorted, terrifying version of itself. I had to get out of there immediately.

Fuelled by the most intense fear I had ever experienced, I frantically abandoned my trolley full of groceries and ran out of the supermarket as quickly as I could manage.

Once in the car park, sitting in my car wrapped in a heavy blanket of abject terror, all I could do was try to catch my breath as my heart raced. *I'm going to faint.* I could not start my car or drive. Frozen in intense fear, I had no idea what was happening to me, but every fibre of my being shouted that it was bad. Life-threatening bad. I needed saving but couldn't save myself since I couldn't move.

The experience of being certain that I was in mortal danger but unable to do anything about it I will never forget. I would not wish that experience or feeling on my worst enemy. Nobody should have to go through that. *Nobody.*

After thirty minutes of what felt like a trip through mental hell, the feelings began to drop in intensity. I was not out of the woods by any stretch, but I could at least start the car and drive away.

I was shaken and still not one hundred per cent right, but thankfully I could limp home after one of the most harrowing experiences of my life.

I arrived home and finally calmed down. I also remained completely confused as to what had just happened. Slowly, I began to shake it off. Over the next few days, I did my best to return to normal day-to-day life.

While I was in the middle of what I now recognise as my first panic attack, I truly thought I was experiencing a medical emergency. You would think I would have run immediately to a doctor to get checked after that episode, but I did not. If I'm being honest, I decided that sticking my head in the sand and ignoring it would make it go away.

I really had no good explanation for what had happened to me, but since I was still standing, I just crossed my fingers and did my best to act like it was all over.

Whatever it was, it was terrifying, but *it should be gone forever, right?*

**As it turns out, it was not over.
It was just getting started.**

It was July of 2016, and unbeknownst to me, I was on the first leg of a two-year journey through a bona fide full-blown anxiety disorder.

Five or six days later, while shopping for clothing, the unthinkable happened. A repeat of what had occurred in the supermarket struck me. Once again, a feeling of unreality descended upon me. The lights in the shop reached that unnaturally bright level. My heart raced as I broke out into an immediate sweat, desperate to take in oxygen. The intense sense of dread and doom returned.

How can this be happening again?!

I needed to escape immediately.

So I did.

In a repeat performance, I fled to the car park and sat, unable to move. I was terrified and frozen. Again.

I began to cry.

Why is this happening to me?

What is wrong with me?

Being afraid and completely confused by one's own body is a vulnerable place to be. My tears were understandable and justified.

Once again, I calmed down enough to get out of my frozen, frightened state. After I got home to the safe zone, I did my best to press on with my life, trying to ignore what was clearly a serious problem.

Two weeks later, at the end of July, the monster caught up with me again. This time I was at work happily typing away at my computer when suddenly my heart started racing. I knew what was happening. All the horrible symptoms, sensations, and thoughts came rushing at me like they had the first two times. That thing was back again. Something was wrong, once more, and I had to run!

I left work immediately, explaining to my manager that something was wrong with me. I told him that I needed medical attention right away, tore out of the office, and headed directly to my doctor's surgery.

This time was worse because now, terrified and confused, I was convinced that something was seriously wrong with me. Normally, I would have had to call ahead and book an appointment to see the doctor. In that situation, calling and waiting for an appointment was absolutely out of the question.

In a very out-of-character move for me, I was aggressive with the doctor's staff. Fear will do that to a person. I insisted in the most emphatic way that my life was in immediate danger and that I needed to see the doctor right then and there. It was clear to everyone that I would not take no for an answer, so I was asked to sit in the waiting room until someone could see me. 'It could be a long wait,' the receptionist said to me as if testing my resolve to sit there. 'That's fine,' I mumbled and found a seat. All the doctors were fully booked that day, but I was told that one would see me when they got a break in their schedule.

When I was called into the doctor's room, I wasted no time reading her a detailed laundry list of all the horrible, terrifying things that were repeatedly happening to my body. They were obviously important and indicative of a major problem. In my mind, she needed to know it all in great, urgent detail. I took extra time to explain how this all happened randomly and out of the blue, which I assumed added to the serious nature of the situation.

Her response?

'I know what this is. This is anxiety.'

I remember thinking *you did not just say that to me. Is she even listening to me? Did she get her medical degree through the mail? Has she lost the plot?*

Anxiety?

Anxiety is what happens when you walk down a dark street in a bad neighbourhood. Anxiety is what you feel when you're stressed or bothered by something. When the attacks hit, I was certainly not stressed or bothered. I'd just been shopping and working. These were not stressful or bothersome things at all. I loved to shop, and I enjoyed my work. *She has to be wrong.*

This was most definitely not 'anxiety,' and I was quite vocal about that.

She countered with the words 'panic attacks'. At that moment, and in the state I was in, she was entirely unconvincing. I immediately brushed her off, deciding that she was way off target.

You see, I thought I knew what a panic attack was. A panic attack is where someone breathes into a paper bag and rolls around on the floor. I'd seen panic attacks in movies and on TV. I *knew* what a panic attack looked like, and this was definitely *not* panic. It looked nothing like any panic attack I had ever seen. I was genuinely terrified, and something was really wrong with me, so what on earth was she talking about? More importantly, *why isn't she going to help me when I could drop dead any minute?*

When confronted with my disbelief and resistance, my doctor pushed back. In retrospect, it was a smart move on her part, and I'm grateful that she did.

She looked at me and said in no uncertain terms, 'No, these are anxiety and panic attacks. I believe they are related to the death of your father. And yes, I reviewed your history before you walked in.'

The death of my father. She said it.

My father died.

Did I leave that part out? I'm sorry. I suppose it's a detail you might need to know.

My father had passed away three months earlier, in April of 2016. Somehow, I had completely ignored this event and the fact that it might impact me in some way.

I loved and adored my father.

I was devastated when he passed, but I did my best to push down my emotions and grief. I remember not crying at his funeral. I remember feeling guilty that I wasn't crying. It felt like I had been placed into a random funeral service because I was so numb. No matter how hard I tried to concentrate on my emotions, I couldn't feel them. The service happened, and I somehow felt and thought nothing about it. I was dissociated from the situation. It was almost like my mind had completely closed the door on any belief that this was really taking place.

I know now that holding all our emotions in and ignoring them is not healthy, but that is what I did. I had done some cursory reading online about grief and loss but really didn't go too deep and try and work through my feelings. In my eyes, my best response to the loss of my father was to get back into my normal routine.

Looking back with some clarity now, I do know that part of this whole anxiety mess was a response to the fact that I felt mostly numb when I lost my dad. I should have been feeling more, but I wasn't. Instead, I was experiencing a very common emotional numbing after a major loss, but I didn't understand that. All I knew was that it felt wrong. I loved my father, so how could I not feel his loss more deeply in my soul? My degree of numbness gave me such shame.

My solution to my shame and to the thought that something was wrong with me emotionally was to bury it and act to the best of my abilities like nothing whatsoever was wrong. That became my standard operating procedure for three months. Even when confronted by my doctor, I was resistant to having to address it in some way. Sitting in her surgery, getting smacked in the face with her words, a big part of me was still sure that just pressing on in denial was the right way to go.

In retrospect, that may have been a miscalculation.

This build-up of stress, loss, and grief became the catalyst for my panic disorder. All my doctor had done was expose it in the most brutal way.

I lost my father; I was experiencing repeated panic attacks, but most importantly, *I was terrified of the next one.* Maybe you can relate? And you probably know where this is going—I was entering the early stages of avoidance—and that was going to make my panic worse.

The doctor then did something that, to this day, makes me laugh. She literally wrote me a prescription for a library book that would help me understand how to deal with panic attacks. Yes, she shoved a piece of paper at me that she had scribbled the name of a book on, and told me to go to the library.

In the moment, I felt like she was dismissing me. There I was, describing what was obviously a serious, horrifying, life-threatening condition, and *she told me to go to the library?*

I suspected that she didn't want to deal with me and was hoping I would not come back. I hung my head as I sat there, trying to understand the idea that what I needed was a book from the library.

Before I got out of the chair, she told me to go to a drop-in lab and get a full blood count done. I guessed she was trying to give me peace of mind by ruling out something physical, but I had heard her say this was anxiety at play.

I left the surgery with my library prescription in hand, shaking my head in disbelief as if I had been sent packing by a professional that was, at best, lacking in compassion and, at worst, entirely incompetent. I'm not saying that she was either of those things, but that is what I was feeling. *She added the blood test out of pity,* I thought as I trudged back out to my car. *When I told her that there was something seriously wrong with me, she didn't care.*

That was fine. I couldn't change her mind, and besides, the prospect of getting the blood tests done was comforting. As I headed home, I convinced myself the blood tests would uncover what was truly wrong. That would prove my doctor wrong. She would see that this wasn't anxiety. Something else was at play. Something serious!

Strangely, as determined as I was to have a blood test prove me right, I put it off. Being convinced I was seriously sick was scary. If I took the blood test, my worst nightmares might come true. In a cruel twist that I would learn is a common issue with an anxiety disorder, I became scared of getting the facts that I also desperately needed.

Disappointed and lost, I was also desperate. As it turns out, that was not a bad motivator in the overall scope of my issues.

Desperation is not something any of us wants to experience. But sometimes, it can be magical. When we are desperate to end our suffering and get answers, we will act. I had no belief in the action I was about to take, but I most definitely needed to do something—anything ...

So I went to the library with her prescription.

If you're going to go to a library, you might as well read.

I did. That's when I began to learn.

CHAPTER 2

ANXIETY SETS UP SHOP

I was ready to learn, but my anxious brain had other ideas.

As I started reading, I found myself getting anxious. The damn book the doctor had prescribed made me anxious. This was both confusing and frustrating for me. The words I read were just words printed on paper but they were triggering my anxiety nonetheless. Now, I was forced to think about anxiety, and that was not going well at all! As I read, my heart started to race. I broke out into a sweat—again.

This was my prescription for anxiety? This was supposed to help?

I was so hopeful that the book would help calm my anxiety, yet it was doing exactly the opposite. I was never an avid reader, so the decision to commit to consuming any book was a big deal for me. The fact that this particular book was a symbol of some hope for me made the situation all the more difficult.

I was anxious, afraid, frustrated, and dejected. I tried to continue reading but finally angrily hurled the book across the room. This was yet another ineffective way for me to 'handle' this anxiety monster that had blown up in my face.

The conclusion I reached at that moment was that I was on my own.

First, I was sure that my doctor was dismissing me. Now the magic book she told me to read was making things worse than they already were. If I was going to beat this thing, I was convinced that I was going to have to find my own way.

It's worth noting that I did finally gather the strength to go for my blood test. The wait for those results was the longest in my life. In reality, it was only three days, but during that time, I was consumed with 'what if' thoughts.

What if it's something life-threatening?

What if I can't be treated?

What if whatever I have is going to kill me?

Unsurprisingly and despite all my catastrophic thinking, my blood levels were fine. Everything was within healthy ranges, and I was told there was no underlying medical condition causing my anxiety.

Was I reassured? Yes. For about twenty minutes, but then that reassurance turned to doubt and more 'what if' thinking.

What if the test results are wrong?

Did they read me the right results?

You hear of mix-ups in the news.

What if I was one of them?

The doctor was no help, the book was no help, and the blood tests were no help. What could I do? I had to push on in some way.

I was about a month into this nightmare, and I was going to be on my own for however long this was going to take.

In retrospect, while I can admire my determination in the face of what felt like an increasingly bleak outlook, I can also see that I was pointing that determination in the wrong direction. In my mind, my two key strategies for going forward would be hope and avoidance.

A few words on that …

HOPE. I hoped with all my might that this dreadful feeling was going to somehow go away. I may have been clinging to the idea that anxiety and panic would dissipate, much like a cold or flu dissipates over time. Well, now, I am aware that this was not much of a strategy. But as tragically passive and misguided as this was, hope was the one thing I could use to keep going.

AVOIDANCE. Up to that point, I had been responding to panic and anxiety by retreating and avoiding, so I thought it best to get really good at that going forward. When I would panic at work, I would retreat to the men's room until I could get it together. If I was out shopping or elsewhere, I would leave the situation I was in the minute I felt anxious. Because I felt better when I did this, I assumed that my job was to now get good at avoiding and escaping as a primary means of managing this monster that was starting to control much of my life.

CONFRONTING MY GRIEF

I should mention that processing the loss of my father in a healthy way did enter the picture. The doctor had strongly suggested that I reach out to a trained grief counsellor to address what had happened. While I had been sceptical when it came to her take on my situation, I was at least open (or desperate) enough to take her advice.

I engaged with a grief counsellor in my area and explored the impact of losing my father. It really was a very smart move. I was ready to talk about it and willing to look at ways to move through it. I didn't stay in grief counselling for that long—only six sessions over a six-week period— but I am so grateful for that handful of sessions.

Just learning about the nature of grief and loss helped me feel better about how I was handling—or avoiding—it. In counselling, I learnt that feeling emotionally numb was a common protective response and nothing to be ashamed of. This was a huge burden lifted off my shoulders! I was given a greater understanding of what loss and grief are all about and some tools I could use to work through them in a normal, healthy way.

If I had only known some of this at the time of my father's passing, my story may have been completely different than the one you are reading now. But I didn't know, and they say that everything happens for a reason, so here we are.

Processing the loss of my father and working through all those emotions was very helpful to me. Carrying all that was not helping in any way with my anxiety and panic problems. I know that for certain. But I would be lying, and this book would be over right here, if I told you that this was a cure for my anxiety disorder. It was not. It was work that needed to be done. Doing it did improve my life and taught me valuable lessons, but I was still tightly gripped by all-day anxiety and recurring panic attacks, so I still had plenty of work to do.

FULL STEAM AHEAD WITH HOPE AND AVOIDANCE

I took my 'hope and avoid' strategy and went head first into my usual daily work routine.

What I wound up experiencing was all-day anxiety, simmering dangerously, always threatening to boil over on me. I tried to hold it at bay, but often it would rise up into a full-blown panic. In those moments in escape mode, I would head to the men's room at work or leave whatever environment I was in.

This was proving to be difficult to sustain.

I was constantly looking over my shoulder and on the run. Anxiety had me on guard every waking moment. I became obsessed with it. All I could think about was my next anxious moment and dreading the next panic attack. I would open my eyes in the morning and immediately begin thinking about how anxious I might be that day. I would lie in bed, terrified, wondering how I was going to make it through another day of constant fear, discomfort, and evasive action. Before I even stood up, I was counting the minutes before I could return home to my safe space.

These thoughts came often, and they were focused on a few main themes.

Maybe today, I will have the worst panic attack ever. Maybe I won't be able to handle it.

Maybe today is the day everyone will see me fall apart in front of them. If that happens, this will get even worse for me.

Maybe this is just a part of me forever. Maybe the entire rest of my life will be full of fear and free of calm or peace.

THE WITCHING HOUR

I struggled through my days for a few months. Hope and avoidance were not working well for me, but I pressed on.

Then something really odd happened.

I had a particularly intense encounter with panic while at work. It hit me while I was on a phone call. I did my best to hold it together, but all I wanted to do was end that call and run. I still had no real idea what I was running from, but running was nearly uncontrollable. After what felt like hours, with my heart pounding and my breath faltering, I was able to end the call.

I ran to the men's room—my safe space—to ride it out, but this episode felt so much more intense than all the others. The symptoms were incredibly strong. The fear was elevated to a level I had not experienced before. It took longer for the panic to subside this time. Even when it did, it wasn't totally over. For the first time, I found myself shaking after the peak of the panic had passed. I was absolutely exhausted mentally, emotionally, and physically.

This panic attack happened at exactly 11 a.m.

Eleven o'clock became my new witching hour. I was literally afraid of that time of day. It was fascinating that one intense panic attack had instantly created an intense fear of the 11 a.m. hour. I found myself fixated on 11 a.m. I dreaded it, obsessed over it, and was beside myself wondering how I was going to make it through that time of day again.

As the clock approached 11 a.m. each day, my anxiety rose. My anxiety and panic symptoms made an appearance as if on cue, often escalating into full-blown panic. I tried to ignore it. I even tried turning off the clock on my computer so I wouldn't see what time it was—to no avail. I continued to experience high anxiety and panic at that time of the day, even when I wasn't exactly sure what time it really was.

I was already doing my best not to drown in a whirlpool of panic but barely keeping my head above the waterline every day. Now I was afraid of the clock too.

How was this even possible?

It felt like there was absolutely nothing I could do to make it better. I was trying, but nothing was working, and I did not understand what was happening to me. Flabbergasted and confused, I was clueless about what to do next. Hoping and wishing it all away with every fibre of my being was not working. Now, anxiety was gluing itself to other parts of my life, including the damn clock. My level of feeling so lost and helpless at that point cannot be measured.

In hindsight, the fact that I knew nothing about the mechanics of anxiety and panic was really showing back then.

NO CHOICE

Every day, I continued to force myself to go to work and grit my teeth through the anxiety. Economically I had no choice, but while I hung onto any semblance of control by my fingernails, I was obsessed with and fixated on how I was feeling. I spent every moment scanning, checking for anxiety, and evaluating my level of fear and discomfort. This continuous state of anticipation had me wrung out, bracing against and fearing the next wave of anxiety or panic attack.

At work, I wasn't terribly productive. To make matters worse, the more exhausted I became fighting this constant anxiety war, the more battles I began to lose.

I WAS NOT ALONE

One day, something unexpected happened. I had no idea at the time because I could not see past my struggles, but what transpired was an incredibly positive turn of events that would have a major impact on my recovery going forward.

I discovered that I was not alone.

Elliot was a work colleague that I got on well with. We were teammates. As teammates sometimes do, we had formed a typical workplace friendship. Having Elliot around made work more fun, but I would not say that we were close friends. We were workmates. I'm sure you know what I'm talking about.

One day Elliot asked me if he could have a word with me.

It was just him and I sitting in the staff room. I don't know if he had seen how anxious I was or if he had had a glimpse of my *Irrational Thoughts* journal (yes, that is the actual title of a journal I used) on my desk, but he knew that I was dealing with something.

'You know,' Elliot said as we faced each other across a table, 'I used to have an anxiety disorder.' My eyes popped wide open at this. For the next few minutes or so, I intently listened as Elliot shared his mental health struggles with me. He confided that he was still a bit of a worrier but that he was no longer gripped by horrible anxiety. He then smiled gently and said, 'I just want you to know that it's okay to talk to me about your mental health. It can make a huge difference.'

I am not ashamed to say that I broke down and cried. 'Thank you, Elliot. You have no idea how much I needed to hear that.' The sense of relief I felt knowing that another human being saw my struggle and wanted to help was amazing. Elliot gave me a hug, I dried my tears, and we went back to work. I *really* needed that hug. I'm not ashamed to say that, either.

That little impromptu meeting was the start of a great friendship and mentorship. Elliot let me talk to him about everything I was thinking and feeling. He listened to my experiences and saw them. He gave me a place to be fully open and honest about my struggle, but more than that, he understood. Elliot had lived it. He knew what it felt like. He also shared his stories with me. It was like he had literally walked in my shoes before I did. It was amazing.

Elliot would become an important part of my recovery story as it unfolded, but for now, I was just trying to take things one day at a time.

SEASONS CHANGE – NOVEMBER 2016

It is a perfectly natural thing for the seasons to change. We all expect it, we all experience it, and sometimes we even celebrate it. But due to the state I was in, the change in seasons signalled yet another problem. When winter arrives in the northern hemisphere, the days grow shorter, and the sun sets earlier. One day in the office, late in the day, I noticed that everything seemed darker. The light had changed. Because something was different, naturally I began to panic.

In short, I noticed the sun was setting. It was right on schedule and completely normal for that time of year, but rather than being a non-issue, this minor development made me wonder if I was about to pass out. As expected, that thought created a flash of fear, which instantly became intense panic. It was so bad that I actually left my workplace because I was so afraid and in such a state.

I tried taking a few days off to recover and come back strong, but that was pointless. When I returned to work, I still experienced the same anxiety and panic every day. Nothing had changed.

How was this possible? Seasons were changing like they always do, but the earlier sunsets were triggering me? Now my panic was happening at 11 a.m. *and* late in the day?

My problems went beyond being at work.

I had also stopped shopping, going out for meals, and engaging in all the things I enjoyed in life. When I did try to do those things, I did them in the grips of extreme anxiety, focused exclusively on the sensations they brought up and the accompanying fear. Every forced outing became a constant mental game of 'will I panic?' There was no joy in any of it. My social life and hobbies were also being taken from me.

I only went shopping when I absolutely had to, and that was just for the basics like food or household supplies. I didn't want to do it this way, but I felt that I had to—as if I had no choice. My world was getting smaller. My existence was increasingly ruled by restrictions, anxiety management rituals, and avoidance behaviours.

This was not okay, and I knew it.

I had to do something.

FALSE START

I was getting frustrated. Very frustrated.

Fuelled by this intense exasperation, I decided that I had to go into a giant shopping centre. I needed to take back at least some of my life, and this was how I was going to do it. Everyone around me was living a normal life, enjoying themselves, and I was desperate to get some of that simple joy back.

> Going into a large shopping centre was my first
> defiant push back against the anxiety monster.

I can see now that this was a totally misguided and under-informed attempt at exposure work. I just didn't know that at the time.

Off I went.

I had the best of intentions.

I also had a series of intense panic attacks while in this giant shopping centre.

These were, like all my other moments of panic, very difficult to handle. I kept trying to grit my teeth and power through it, but the panic kept coming at me each time.

Knowing that I was going to panic at this level at the shops triggered a change in my overall anxiety pattern. Previously, the anxiety and panic had been confined to the shops, but slowly I found myself getting anxious even driving towards a shopping centre. This was new, and it was not the positive development I was hoping for. I was supposed to be getting less anxious. Instead, I was getting more anxious in more situations.

My misguided attempt to take my life back had backfired on me.

As a result, my avoidance kicked into an even higher gear.

The anxiety.

The fear.

The panic.

It was ruling my life. I was no longer in control of my days.

Rapidly, I was becoming a frightened shell of myself—on a downward spiral.

What am I supposed to do to make this end? I would think with tears in my eyes. I had no defence against this monster. The tools that I thought would work weren't doing anything but somehow making me worse.

My life got smaller and smaller by the day. This was no way to live. What started as a single panic attack in July had grown into a deteriorating existence by January.

I had lived this way, being terrified and gripped by anxious thoughts and symptoms, for a full six months. There seemed to be no stopping it. I had no escape route. On most days, I was convinced this was how the rest of my years were going to look.

I felt so alone.

The doctor was no help on my first visit in August.

Since I had so quickly discarded the book she had asked me to read, and my blood tests said I was healthy, I couldn't return to her for fear of being berated or even thrown out of the surgery.

None of my strategies were working.
Hoping was pointless.
Avoidance was ineffective.

None of my attempts to control my anxiety and panic were even remotely close to successful.

I was getting worse, and I was out of options.

CHAPTER 3

WHAT DID IT LOOK LIKE?

Before I move on to talk about my 'enough is enough' moment, and what I did that actually worked, I want to answer a question I get asked all the time by the DLC Anxiety community.

'Did you have (insert symptom here)?'

When I was in the midst of my anxiety disorder, knowing that I was not the only person feeling what I was feeling became a real lifeline for me. None of us wants to be alone in the world. We definitely don't want to be alone in our suffering. One of the most rewarding aspects of my life today—after anxiety—is watching the DLC community help people feel not so alone.

I'd like to take this short chapter to describe some of the symptoms and thoughts that stalked me while I was suffering.

I can't list every anxiety symptom in the world. That would require a book far longer than this one, but I can share with you my most common symptoms in the hope that you may not feel so isolated.

I'll describe each of my common symptoms as I experienced them and will attempt to provide a basic explanation of those symptoms. As part of my eventual recovery, accessing well-respected vetted sources of psychoeducation was important. Those sources explained my symptoms to me. They helped me understand that while I was interpreting what I was feeling as dangerous, these symptoms were really not. I'll do my best to pass some of that along to you here.

I must remind you that you should not use this book to diagnose medical conditions or inform treatment in the event of actual medical problems. The information I am sharing is general in nature and is meant solely to inform at a basic level.

PANIC SYMPTOMS

Feeling of impending doom If pressed, I would probably say that this was the most difficult panic symptom for me to handle. During a panic attack, the feeling that I was in great danger and subject to a rush of impending doom was completely overwhelming. The feeling was so intense I was convinced something terrible was about to happen, even if I could not identify exactly what it was. This feeling told me to immediately run and escape. It was almost impossible to resist. While logically I know that I was never in any real danger during my panic attacks, this terrible feeling that I came to dread was quite convincing when it told me otherwise.

Explaining the feeling of impending doom If panic is a response to a perceived threat, then it makes sense that I would feel like something was about to go horribly wrong. Without a terrible impending outcome, we could surmise, without knowing better, that there would be no threat. When we panic, we are reacting to a threat that does not exist, yet our brains will insist that something is wrong. We can't find that something because it's not real, but that does not matter to our brains in the heat of the moment. We are responding to a perceived threat condition. That response tells us that things are going wrong and that we must escape to stay out of harm's way. Even though the threat is never real, the perception of it is more than enough to trigger evasive action.

Racing heart My panic attacks always included a racing heart. In a few short seconds, it felt like my heart went from its normal beating to pounding out of my chest. It was terrifying. I was afraid not only of the speed at which my heart was beating but also of the force of each beat. Both racing and pounding are quite accurate descriptions of the sensations I experienced in my heart.

Explaining the racing heart Escaping from a dangerous situation requires us to move our bodies and expend physical energy. If you've ever jogged down your street, you know to accommodate that energy expenditure, our hearts will speed up to meet the demand for increased oxygen delivery and waste product removal. My galloping heart certainly felt anything but normal, but in reality, it was working exactly as it was designed to do during those panic attacks.

Derealisation When I would experience derealisation, the world would suddenly look different to me. Not just different, but wrong. Things or environments that were usually familiar would take on an odd, almost foreign, feel. Places and people I knew well felt strange and different to me. When in the middle of derealisation, I struggled to accurately process what I was seeing around me. Faces looked weird. It also felt like everyone was looking at me, even though I knew logically they were not. Sounds were distorted and unfamiliar. The world sometimes felt like it was moving in slow motion. This was such an uncomfortable and terrifying feeling. Derealisation was so extreme and wrong that I was certain it was signalling a serious problem of some kind, either physically or psychologically. Derealisation made me feel like I was right at the edge of insanity.

Explaining derealisation I have heard derealisation explained as a 'circuit breaker' of sorts. When faced with extreme danger, fear, or stress, the mind triggers this state as a way to separate us from intense feelings— much like a circuit breaker does. This is a protective measure, although it felt far from protective to me. I have passed this explanation on to members of the DLC community who are struggling with derealisation. Often, they will respond incredulously, believing strongly that nothing that feels so terrifying and dangerous could possibly be designed to serve a useful purpose. I completely understand that. Really, I do.

I have come to think that maybe this state really did help our ancestors in some way. When feeling like the environment was slowing, I could focus on small body language gestures and cues that one might miss in a normal state. Maybe the noise distortion was my ears adjusting to a higher frequency. I can't be sure, but if I think about derealisation in terms of the fight-or-flight response, this makes some kind of sense to me.

Light Sensitivity From my very first panic attack, being sensitive to light and seeing the world as suddenly much brighter was at the top of my symptoms list. When my anxiety reached the tipping point on the way to panic, lights instantly flared brighter than they had been just a few seconds ago. Seeing the world get instantly brighter without being able to explain why seemed to indicate something being terribly wrong with my eyes or brain. As you would expect, this interpretation instigated excessive amounts of fear.

Explaining light sensitivity When we are afraid or facing a threat, our pupils naturally dilate. They open wider. This is regulated by our autonomic nervous system and is beyond our control. Wider pupils mean more light entering the eye. Learning that this was a natural part of the fight-or-flight response (or really any state of arousal) helped me take my first steps towards real recovery. Knowing why the world was suddenly brighter didn't instantly stop my panic or anxiety, but it did help me change the way I reacted to it.

Hyperventilation (over-breathing and panting) When anxious and in a state of panic, I would struggle to breathe properly. Often I would pant, breathing very rapidly and in a shallow manner. This would lead to feeling lightheaded and dizzy. This state added fear on top of an already scary situation.

Explaining hyperventilation Part of fight-or-flight is rapid breathing. If we are engaged in actual fighting or running, breathing rapidly serves an important purpose. When we are NOT engaged in fighting or running, the result of rapid breathing is too little carbon dioxide in the bloodstream and too much oxygen. When this balance is disrupted, the outcome is lightheadedness, dizziness, tingling, and other unpleasant feelings. If you have ever experienced this, you know what I'm talking about.

Sweating When my anxiety spilled over into full panic, I began to sweat as if someone had turned on a switch in my body. One second I was fine. The next, I would feel myself perspiring all over. This would happen to me out of the blue while I was sitting or standing still. That made it scary because I interpreted sweating without moving as an indicator that something was really wrong with me.

Explaining sweating Sweating is an important part of temperature regulation. In a situation where we are required to flee or take physical action to remain safe, our bodies will sweat to keep us cool while we expend energy. Sweating while wrestling with an alligator would have felt normal to me. Sweating while purchasing a pint of milk was not expected or required, so it naturally added fuel to my panic fire.

Hypersensitive hearing My panic attacks usually included what felt like superhearing! I became very sensitive to every sound in my environment. Everything seemed louder and sharper to me, which translated immediately to 'scarier'!

Explaining hypersensitive hearing While it certainly felt like my hearing ability was elevated to superhero levels, the best explanation I was given for this was focused more on the fact that my brain was working overtime to detect and process sounds as part of the effort to keep me safe. In times of real danger, awareness of our environment becomes vital, so being keenly focused on every sound in the room was just my brain doing what it thought I needed it to do at that moment.

GENERAL BACKGROUND ANXIETY SYMPTOMS

Sometimes it felt like I was always in a state of panic, but I wasn't. However, even when I was not feeling this way, I was always in a state of elevated anxiety. I wasn't only dealing with panic symptoms but with a continuous stream of general, always there, simmering-in-the-background anxiety and anxiety symptoms.

This always-on background anxiety caused some uncomfortable and distressing physical symptoms.

I experienced stomach and gastrointestinal symptoms quite often. It was common for me to have to stay close to a bathroom due to IBS-like issues. I experienced quite a bit of bloating, or at least what felt like bloating. Stomach-related issues are quite common with anxiety and, unfortunately for me, that held 100 per cent true.

I also experienced a tremendous amount of tension in my muscles and all over my body. This was especially prevalent in my head, neck, jaw, and shoulders. If I was awake, I was tense.

I developed a twitch in my left leg. Random, unexplainable (at the time) muscle twitches in my leg became the norm for me. I had never experienced twitching before, but being in a continuous anxious state caused this ever-present new symptom. Curiously, at one point, the twitch moved from my left leg to my right leg, which, as you can imagine, was also quite confusing and a bit unnerving.

I could go on listing symptoms for page after page, but that is not the focus of this story. I just wanted to acknowledge some of my more prevalent symptoms and share the helpful explanations I found when I really needed them. My hope is that you will find them helpful too.

WHAT ABOUT YOUR SYMPTOMS?

You may be experiencing symptoms that I have not listed. That is okay and to be expected. Not everyone experiences the same anxiety symptoms. If I did not mention a symptom here, it does not mean it does not exist. It certainly may, and it may for a large number of people. Just not for me. Do not interpret my omission of your particular symptom(s) as an indicator of anything in particular.

ABOUT SYMPTOM-FOCUSED PSYCHOEDUCATION

Learning what my anxiety symptoms were and why they were happening was important for me. I had been interpreting the bodily sensations of anxiety and panic as dangerous and threatening, but I was wrong. Learning that they were both natural and safe was a major factor in how I changed my view on addressing a problem that previously seemed completely unsolvable.

The realisation that my symptoms were not harmful was a bit frustrating because it felt so opposite to what I was feeling, but this realisation was sorely needed. My symptom-focused psychoeducation became a bit of an extended eureka moment in my recovery. There were tearful moments as I learnt I was not broken and that my body was not damaged. I found hope in that knowledge, small though it was at times.

Nonetheless, I must acknowledge that learning about my symptoms didn't change everything for me. I wasn't instantly better. It made me less confused and gave me my first somewhat firm ground to stand on, but I was soon to find out that just *knowing* would not be enough. Yes, I was educated and no longer as confused about my symptoms as before, but the anxiety, fear, and avoidance were still there. The panic attacks still hit me. I continued to struggle day in and day out.

Even so, this was just the first chapter of my healing. I was to learn there was far more to my story than researching symptoms.

We'll get to that shortly.

First, let me tell you about the different forms my anxiety took over time.

CHAPTER 4

MY ANXIETY OVERLAP

I promise I am going to get to the part where I find my way out of panic and anxiety hell. But before we go over that, I want to take a few more minutes to answer another common question.

Quite often, in the DLC Anxiety community, I am asked if I only had panic attacks. Many members of the community want to know if there was more to what I was battling than that.

Did I have intrusive thoughts?

Did I have health anxiety?

Was I afraid to drive or leave the house?

One of the benefits of belonging to a large mental health and well-being community is that we get to learn from each other and find inspiration and encouragement in the knowledge that we are not alone. In the spirit of the DLC community, I'm happy to talk about this here before we move on.

My anxiety journey was rooted in more than just panic attacks and panic disorder. There was clear and persistent overlap with other forms of disordered anxiety.

Panic attacks were undoubtedly the worst part of the experience for me. They were the scariest and hardest to handle aspect of my struggles with an anxiety disorder. But this did not make them the only ingredient of my anxiety problem. Far from it.

Like most people who suffer from an anxiety disorder, I experienced different manifestations of anxiety and fear. These manifestations can come in different forms, including:

1.   Generalised anxiety

2.   Health anxiety

3.   Agoraphobia

There are certainly more. Social anxiety and obsessive–compulsive disorder (OCD) are two of the most common forms of disordered anxiety spoken about in the DLC Anxiety community. Eating disorders can often exist alongside problems like panic disorder and OCD. Depression is another common overlapping condition alongside panic attacks, panic disorder, and other forms of anxiety disorders. I didn't experience these conditions in my journey, but they certainly do exist and impact people every day.

As I go over my own overlapping conditions, please keep in mind that my experience was not and is not representative of the entire range of anxiety conditions or states. The fact that I may not have experienced the same overlapping condition(s) that you experience does not invalidate your experience or indicate that something is wrong, or worse, about your situation.

Remember, always consult a qualified health care or mental health professional when seeking clarification on your own well-being.

GENERALISED ANXIETY

Generalised anxiety was a major component for me. Persistent background anxiety and panic attacks often come together. Unfortunately, I was no exception to this combination.

There was almost no relief from my generalised anxiety. It was quite distressing. The constant background anxiety at a low boil all day long made it near impossible to work or even leave the house. Everything became a huge struggle for me. Being anxious all the time made me feel so fragile too.

If I was awake, I felt anxiety at varying degrees. I was caught in the trap of monitoring my level of anxiety all the time and watching it slowly creep up throughout the day. This triggered an intense worry that the anxiety would become full-blown panic, which terrified me. This low level of anxiety all day long also meant that my stress tolerance level was decreased on most days to the point where simple work tasks like meetings or phone calls became difficult for me to tolerate. I was so on edge and so tuned into my anxiety in every waking minute that it felt to me as if I could simply not handle what I needed to do.

Such a disposition poured fuel on the fire of my already anxious brain, causing my anxiety level to spike repeatedly. This often resulted in full panic attacks that nearly brought me to my knees several times every day.

It may be possible for a person to experience panic disorder without being anxious between attacks, but I can say with 100 per cent certainty that I was not that person.

HEALTH ANXIETY

Health anxiety was another big problem for me, alongside my panic disorder. I was intently focused on what was happening in my body and afraid of my sensations. I quickly developed the habit of interpreting these sensations as health emergencies and health threats. This triggered all kinds of checking and safety rituals—including spending far too much time with Doctor Google.

Whenever I would experience scary anxiety symptoms, I would run to Google and search for them, trying to determine if something was really wrong with me or if my life was in actual danger. Anyone who has ever developed this habit will tell you it never goes well. Googling my symptoms became a major obstacle to any forward progress in my recovery.

For instance, I would sit myself down at my computer and search for 'fast, racing heart'.

Google, being Google, was happy to show me a mountain of information related to rapid heartbeat. There, among those search results, were *real* heart conditions and cardiac problems. This was exactly *not* what an anxious, fear-driven brain needs to see. In the state I was in, I would immediately latch onto the scariest, most serious heart-related health conditions Google displayed, certain that I needed to know more to save myself.

To make matters worse, my father had a history of heart disease. There were multiple heart attacks and strokes and I grew up always aware of his issues. So much so that when I was young I would often lie awake at night waiting for him to come home, and worried that he might not make it because of his health problems. At times, I would even leave the house in the middle of the night to go looking for him, my mind fixated on the image of him collapsed on the pavement.

My father's heart problems did contribute to his passing, so this really was an issue for me.

I did know that I am not my father, but do you think my anxious brain knew that? Of course not. My sensitised mind took my father's heart issues and immediately glued them to my own anxiety symptoms.

It convinced me that my family medical history was coming to get me and that something was seriously wrong with my heart as a result.

The more I read and searched, the more anxious and afraid I became, which then drove me to read and search even more in a desperate attempt to find safety and assurance. It was a terrible cycle that accomplished nothing but made me even more anxious and afraid. Researching my symptoms did not save me from any real health problems. All it did was delay my recovery and keep me stuck for some time.

One thing I learnt along the way was that while we might jokingly call it *Doctor Google*, Google is most certainly not a doctor and is not a good source of medical advice.

Google might be a rich source of medical information, but information without proper application is not advice. *Google is designed to show us popular information, not necessarily accurate or appropriate diagnostic information.* Remember this if you feel tempted to do a search on your symptoms.

When I would sit down and perform a frantic search to verify that my symptoms were or were not about to kill me, I did not get results that matched my situation at all. I only got a collection of links that Google identified as popular. But because they were, I assumed they would help me.

Oh, Google.

How could a bunch of people who were so smart be so off the mark at the same time?

If I can pass along anything from my health anxiety struggle, it would be to stay far away from Doctor Google. If you're already in a relationship with ol' Doc Google, fire it today. Get your advice from an actual doctor who can perform real medical tests and make an accurate assessment of your individual needs.

In a somewhat cruel twist, I found myself also terrified to go to a real doctor!

I struggled to take the advice I just gave you because I was so convinced that I had a serious heart condition.

The idea of getting tested was terrifying. I was sure the news I would receive would be horrible and that my doom would be confirmed. It took me quite a while to get up the courage to bring my heart concerns to the doctor.

Waiting to get my test results—which took a full week—was excruciating. I spent every day that week an anxious, worried mess.

Finally, the test results came in, and it was good news! There was nothing wrong with my heart. All my fear and worry were for nothing.

My anxious brain was relieved. For a few minutes. It then told me that the doctor may have missed something; my good news was not good news at all. All that effort and all that waiting and worrying got me a few minutes of relief before I discarded what the doctor had told me. My new angle was assuming they were wrong, so I went right back into the panic and anxiety cycle for quite a while.

This was exhausting and frustrating, to say the least.

It wasn't just my heart that I worried was secretly betraying me; I fixated on what my muscle twitches really meant. I then went through the same mental song and dance with the twitches as my heart. Being afraid of them. Googling them. Getting worked up into an emotional lather. Checking with a doctor. Getting medical assurance that I was fine. And finally, disregarding that assurance based on the idea that the doctors could be wrong.

This merry-go-round went on and on as I followed the process from one symptom to the next. It felt like someone was playing a cruel joke on me. I'd finally get a handle on one scary symptom then another would take its place. I was sure that it would never end.

While panic attacks were the scariest part of my anxiety journey, my health anxiety patterns were the most detrimental. The continued cycle of checking, scanning, verifying, asking, confirming, then doubting and repeating kept me stuck for longer than I had to be.

BREAKING THE CYCLE OF HEALTH ANXIETY

I realise I just told you not to use Google to seek assurance and safety, but at the same time, I have to be honest about what ultimately helped me break the Google habit. In hindsight, I can't believe I didn't do this right from the start. Out of frustration, when I was Googling, I started including the word 'anxiety'. Instead of seeing only popular search results about actual medical conditions, Google would show me sites that, in many cases, explained that what I was experiencing was very common anxiety symptoms.

These explanations, combined with the constant assurance I extracted from my doctors, was enough to allow me to slowly break my symptom checking and symptom-focusing habit. It was far from easy, but I had to start doing something different with my health anxiety. As it turns out, this little change in my googling habits was one catalyst that helped me start to move in a new direction.

AGORAPHOBIA

I also struggled with agoraphobia and agoraphobic tendencies.

Many people think that agoraphobia is just the fear of leaving one's house or bedroom. But agoraphobia is more than that.

Agoraphobia is the fear of being in a situation that may trigger anxiety or even panic. That might be leaving the house. It might be driving or being in a shopping centre. It might be sitting in a restaurant or in the chair at the dentist's office. This fear manifests in many different places and situations for many different people.

My agoraphobia was based on the initial fear of being in a shopping centre. As I've recounted, going into a shopping centre was virtually guaranteed to result in a panic attack for me. So I instantly developed a fear of those places. The more I tried to push through, the more I would panic. Then an odd thing happened.

Whenever I would even try to go to a shopping centre, the panic would appear earlier and earlier in my trip. I would panic simply *arriving* at the shopping centre. I no longer had to even go in to trigger panic. Then I would panic *on the drive* to the shopping centre. Next, I would get anxious or even panic *before I even got into the car* to drive to the shopping centre. When it came to associating panic and anxiety with specific places, then avoiding them, I couldn't deny it was getting worse over time.

The fear of being inside a shopping centre expanded into other situations. Before long, the places where I felt safe got fewer. This is a textbook example of how agoraphobia develops from panic disorder. I know now that I was absolutely going down that path.

TRIGGERING THE NEED FOR CHANGE

Panic is certainly impactful in a life. Constant anxiety is a struggle. Health anxiety can become a torturous cycle that can disrupt many aspects of life. Agoraphobia seems downright tragic. It is the ultimate fear-based restriction of an otherwise healthy and normal life. If I am being fully honest, the idea of being agoraphobic was absolutely terrifying, but I was toying with that path.

This was a fate I could not accept.

The clear march towards becoming homebound—or even worse—acted as a major shove to get me to the 'enough is enough' point in my journey. I was not in any way interested in becoming stuck in my house. It was time to make a serious change.

CHAPTER 5

ENOUGH IS ENOUGH: THE TURN OF THE TIDE

I was completely sick and tired of battling through each day. It felt like I was just surviving rather than living. One moment stands out in particular. I thought to myself, *I CANNOT DO THIS ANY MORE!*

In hindsight, I can see that I had to be *ready* to learn before I could begin to truly learn. By this point, I was absolutely resigned to doing whatever would work. In my desperation, I was ready to hear what I needed to—anything to get better and move out of my personal hell.

Remember the library book that my doctor asked me to read? I had thrown that book across my room in anger and could not bear to read it because it was making me so anxious and uncomfortable. Well, I went back to that book. It may have been sheer desperation that motivated me, but I borrowed the book from the library again. This time, I was determined to read it and prayed that it contained the answers that would break me loose from my misery.

I managed to get through the entire thing this time. It really was a bit of a godsend. The book taught me what my symptoms were and, more importantly, *why* they were plaguing me. Understand, it did not cure me by any stretch of the imagination, but it provided me with much-needed information that would become the first block in the foundation of my recovery.

I also worked up the courage to go back to the doctor. Since I had read the book, it felt like I could step foot in her surgery again. I'd been afraid that once I'd confessed I had not read the book, she would dismiss me and maybe even refuse to help me. I had been feeling like a classic case of 'the guy who refuses to help himself'. But after consuming the book, I was ready.

As it turns out, all my fear was misguided and misplaced. I was *very* good at misguided and misplaced fear in those days, wasn't I?

My doctor could not have been nicer to me. She understood why I was afraid to read the book. She listened as I told her how I had struggled since we had last met. The judgement and dismissal I feared so much never came. Instead, I was offered a compassionate ear and what would prove to be some excellent advice and information.

I was pointed to the official NHS (National Health Service) website. Specifically, I was told to access NHS information regarding cognitive behavioural therapy (CBT). One thing we have going for us in the UK is the NHS. It is not without its flaws, but for me, it became a critical source of excellent psychoeducation I could rely on. The book the doctor suggested and the information provided by the NHS allowed me to finally piece together a recovery strategy.

THINGS BEGIN TO CHANGE

Over the next six months, I immersed myself in information, education, and research. It was encouraging to note that I was slowly starting to change my direction, but at first there was very little actual forward movement. This time involved me reading everything I could find on anxiety disorders and effective treatment, but it took a while to actually put into practice some of what I was reading.

I may have been hoping that just knowing would be enough. I can acknowledge that possibility. But I'm reasonably sure at this point that I was simply following a path that so many sufferers do.

We fight.

Then we deny.

Then we learn.

Then we do.

In the DLC Anxiety community, I see this sequence play out, again and again, every day. Because of this, I know that between March and June, I was moving from denial to learning.

In June or July, I started taking tiny steps into the doing zone, trying to apply what I had been reading. When I say the steps were tiny, I am not exaggerating. I was still clearly afraid to poke the beast too hard, so I was tentative. In those first few months, I dipped my toe in the water, not yet ready to dive all the way in.

Still, I was starting to see change. It was small change and, on some days, barely perceptible, but it was happening. At last, I was moving in the direction of recovery.

Throughout this whole period, I had been regularly sharing my struggle with Elliot and chatting with him about his journey, anxiety, and recovery in general. He was very generous with his time and his advice and was a kind and compassionate guide—something I really needed back then.

Alongside all the reading and learning I was doing, Elliot was a tremendous resource and a source of much-needed support for me.

He would invite me around to grab a bite, watch a movie, or do what mates do, but often we would talk about anxiety, mental health, and the tools that worked for him—although they were not working for me.

More than anything else, Elliot made me see that I was not unique in my suffering. He gave me the hope I needed, holding a torch I could follow when in the dark. I will never have enough words to describe the impact Elliot's support had on me. It was immeasurable.

One day, Elliot suggested that we start walking at lunch rather than just sitting in the staff room. We would walk, eat, and chat about whatever popped into our heads. Sometimes we talked about mental health or how we were feeling. Other times we talked about nothing in particular like regular lads will do.

Those walks became an important part of my recovery. They helped me bring down my anxiety levels and gave me a midday boost that helped me get through the second half of my workday. My background anxiety levels continued to drop at work. I found myself not needing to take those little breaks so often, and I was not ending the day full of tension and muscle aches. This was the shift I had been waiting for; I began to look forward to going home and doing something relaxing that I knew was good for my well-being.

But as expected, I knew there would be tough days and setbacks.

LET'S KEEP THIS A SECRET

Not everyone is completely in tune with mental health issues. One moment I will share next sadly illustrates this point.

From the very start, I kept my anxiety issues a secret at work. I asked for time off here and there but provided few details as to why I needed it. Honestly, I was ashamed and embarrassed to tell anyone in my workplace about what I was going through. My feelings alone made me feel weak and out of control, so speaking to my managers or co-workers about them wasn't desirable. *Will they see me differently if I share what's really going on? Will I lose my job because they think I'm a weak cog?*

In the spring of 2017, I moved to a new place of employment. I took with me my work experience, my work skills, my work talents—and my still evolving anxiety disorder.

But I was worried about making this change. I really did not want to mess things up by trying to hide my anxiety issues, so a month or two into the new job, I got up the courage to talk to my managers about my situation. I had not planned to completely open up to them about every detail, but I was starting to see some progress and needed some space at work to move that along. In my mind, it couldn't be avoided if I was to keep getting better. Holding onto my secret and disappearing into the men's room so often (yes, I was still doing that) wasn't a great way to spend the day at work. I had to address my situation with my superiors, at least on a baser level.

During the meeting I had called, I told my managers what I was experiencing—that I was struggling with anxiety—but that I was work-ing on it. 'So …' I asked in a soft voice, 'Do you think it would be okay for me to take short breaks to gather myself when needed here and there?' I paused for a minute to assess my managers' expressions. They looked at me intently, but their eyes appeared empathetic, so I went on. 'You know, I might need to just go outside for some air or otherwise leave my work table for a few minutes if things get a bit too intense.' Waiting for them to respond was like mentally chewing my fingernails. Bringing the subject up had not been easy for me. It was even more difficult to ask for a special consideration for something I felt so ashamed of—and in a new job to boot!

To my relief, my managers smiled and said they understood. One spoke up and said, 'Sure, and we have no problem with what you're asking. You can take little breaks when needed.'

Internally, I unleashed the mother of all pent-up sighs. Getting a positive response was the best possible outcome.

But that wasn't the end of the conversation. After telling me that it was fine to take breaks when needed, my manager sprang a surprise on me. 'Let's go ahead and keep this to ourselves, okay?'

My smile disappeared even as I nodded my head at him.

A secret.
It has to be a secret.

This was a huge punch in the stomach for me. Suddenly, I felt weak and out of control again. I had to ask for special permission to take short work breaks because I could not handle my anxiety. Yes, that permission was granted but being told to keep things quiet was just confirmation (in my head) that my problem was a sign of weakness that nobody else should be allowed to see.

I left the meeting not feeling relieved and supported but humiliated and discouraged. I had been granted room to take breaks when I needed but told to hide it. In my estimation, this was not a good development. I had been making progress in my recovery, but my confidence took a hit that day. I needed some time to shake it off and get it back.

When I look back at this moment, I don't think that my managers meant to say anything bad to me. They were trying to help in whatever way they thought they could. They had no problem accommodating me but didn't understand the implications of how they had granted my request.

They didn't know that asking me to intentionally hide my condition from the rest of the company would strike such an emotional blow.

I can't really blame them for not knowing, but that doesn't negate the emotional setback I had to overcome.

In the DLC Anxiety community, we talk all the time about raising awareness and breaking the stigma associated with mental health issues. I know my passion for this topic is in large part rooted in this leg of my recovery journey.

7 OCTOBER

By the autumn of 2017, I just needed a big win to bolster my confidence. I wasn't totally sinking any more, which was great, but I wasn't really making great progress either. I was like a struggling football club that can't seem to get on track, and that needs one strong match to end a mediocre streak.

My father's birthday was 7 October. It's always a difficult day for me—a day full of memories and feelings of loss and grief. This was the second birthday since his passing eighteen months prior. The first birthday was an occasion that I marked with ... nothing. I have a hard time understanding that, but I was still so emotionally numb and refusing to address my loss that I let his first birthday pass with barely an acknowledgment. I know now that this was at least part of my problem.

That 7 October, however, something was different.

When I opened my eyes that morning, I just got out of bed and got ready to go to work. I did not get lost in the usual thoughts about how terrible the day was going to be. I did not get swept away by the fear. I managed to steer clear of the usual obsessive focus of what was ahead for me anxiety-wise.

Maybe I was trying to make my father proud of me on his birthday. Maybe the emotions of the day pushed me enough to make a difference.

I really don't know what it was that made a difference for me that morning, but I needed that short break in that moment. Regardless of what the catalyst was, I will never forget that on 7 October—my father's birthday—I took my first small *lasting* steps towards recovery.

**It wasn't a huge step.
It was a small change.
But it mattered.**

An hour or so one autumn morning where I wasn't completely terrified of my life made all the difference in my healing trajectory.

That day at work, I went to the NHS website and researched CBT and how it was used to treat anxiety disorders. I wasn't sure that it was going to work for me, but I was at least calm enough that day to give it a chance.

One of the CBT tools I discovered in my research that day was journaling targeted at anxious, irrational thoughts.

My mind was always full of these thoughts. They told me that I was going to be anxious and that every sensation would be terrifying and horrible. They reminded me that I would panic at 11 a.m. and suggested I would never make it all the way to 5 p.m. and the end of the workday. My thoughts were demons, telling me that I was in danger and that I might never break free of this monster ruining my life.

The NHS website told me that I should consider getting those thoughts out of my head and into the world in some way. The instructions told me to write them down, then pair them with more rational thoughts. I decided to give it a try. After all, I had nothing to lose.

I took the most common thoughts—my anxious brain's highlight reel—and put them on paper. Then I paired each of those horrible thoughts with more rational thoughts.

For example:

Irrational Thought: *What if I have a massive panic attack at eleven o'clock?*

Rational Thought: *Even if I do have a panic attack at eleven, I've been having them for eighteen months, and they always seem to end without me dying or going insane.*

Irrational Thought: *What if the anxiety keeps building all day and it gets so bad that I can't handle it by 5 p.m.?*

Rational Thought: *The anxiety has been going up and down every day for a very long time now, and it has never been so bad that it permanently broke me.*

This little exercise seemed like nothing much to me, but as the day went on, I noticed something different.

My anxiety level was still high, but it wasn't what it usually was. It didn't feel like it was continuously building to some horrible fever pitch. It was uncomfortable. It was there. But it felt a little less unbearable for the first time in a very long time.

Was I cured?

Absolutely not.
But this very small change made another difference in my progress.

53

I went back to my 'cognitive reframing' sketchbook and wrote something else.

I did this cognitive reframing exercise and it worked! I feel better today than I have in a very long time. It really worked.

It was important for me to record that. Up to that point, almost everything anxiety-related in my head was negative and catastrophic in nature. I needed to see something positive and this was it. Writing a few thoughts made me feel a little better, so I wanted to write down more thoughts! In particular, I wanted to write positive thoughts. That felt critical in that moment. Maybe it was. Maybe it wasn't. Either way, I will never forget writing that little positive acknowledgement in that sketchbook.

When I arrived home at the end of that day—7 October, my father's birthday—I felt so good and proud of myself. I had tried a thing that was supposed to help me— and it did! I cannot begin to tell you how impactful that experience was for me. For the first time, I felt like maybe I had a way to get out of the hole I was in. For the first time in a very long time, I felt flashes of positivity.

This was the first eureka moment in my recovery. It came on 7 October.

Thank you, Dad.

GETTING IT OUT OF MY HEAD

Over the next few months, I continued the practice of writing down my anxious and irrational thoughts. When I would have a thought, I would write it down. Amazingly, I was experiencing a gradual drop in my overall anxiety levels. It felt like life was finally on the upswing. Taking those thoughts and putting them on paper—getting them outside of my own mind—was helping to lower their intensity and the fear my unexpressed thoughts were triggering. Writing down my irrational thoughts and countering them with more rational thoughts did not instantly stop them. Far from it, but it gave me new ways to act and relate to my thoughts differently. I didn't feel like I was being tossed around uncontrollably by my mind whenever it felt like it.

However, nothing is perfect.
We all know this to be true, but we generally want to
ignore this inconvenient truth whenever possible.

The flaw in my plan came to light one day on a walk with a friend. During our walk, I realised that I did not have my journal pad with me. Instantly, my anxiety level rose. Knowing that I had no way to write down my thoughts was fuelling fear. I was afraid and not sure what to do.

I wrestled with my rising anxiety and tried to come to grips with the fact that my journal was not available just then. I turned to my friend and told him that I was feeling quite anxious. I'm not sure why I did that, but I did. Curiously, the minute I told him how I was feeling, my anxiety level began to come down. It didn't disappear, but it did decrease.

Interesting.

Not having my journal available, and knowing that I could not get the scary thoughts out of my head made me anxious. But in that moment, I learnt that telling my friend I was anxious lowered my anxiety level. The simple act of speaking my thoughts into the open had a positive effect on my mental state. My anxiety and fear decreased enough to be noticeable. Write the thoughts; feel better. Speak the thoughts; feel better. *Make a note of that, Dean.*

As the weeks passed, I continued doing what seemed to be working for me. When I could write down my irrational, anxious thoughts, I did. But after that first incident on the walk with my friend, I did a little more digging into how journaling and reframing fit into CBT for anxiety disorders. Sure enough, it is not news that sometimes a journal becomes a crutch. That was a little light bulb moment in my recovery. The practice of writing my thoughts as soon as I had them had become a safety behaviour. I knew it was having a positive impact, but I was also seeing it as an escape hatch from my anxiety. My ability to cope with feeling anxious became dependent on my ability to write in my journal pad. What happened on my walk illustrated that point. So while it was a bit of a scary moment for me, it was also an important moment.

That moment taught me that it wasn't so much the act of writing on paper as it was the releasing of my thoughts into a space outside my head.

Write them. Speak them. Both produced a small but predictable drop in anxiety levels and helped me avoid falling into the anxiety and panic spiral that had gripped me for so long.

I modified my routine so that if I had my journal with me, I would write down what I was thinking. If I was out and did not have my journal with me, I would simply tell my friends or family members that I was feeling anxious.

You may be thinking that automatically telling people that I was anxious and afraid could have been hard on my relationships. I was quite fortunate in that it really was not. I think there are two reasons why my practice of speaking about how I was feeling did not turn out badly with respect to my friends and family members.

When I shared my feelings, the unloading was merely a relief valve. I might tell everyone at a family gathering that I was feeling very anxious in a given moment, but I did not demand or require a response. I was just letting it out of my head. Not making any particular demands kept the pressure off everyone.

Beyond that, I am fortunate to have great people around me in my life. While I didn't need any special words from anyone when I would express my anxiety verbally, I naturally hoped I would be supported. Support doesn't always mean 'fix me'. Sometimes support means patience, understanding, acceptance, and assurance that your friends are on your side. That is exactly what I received.

Expressing myself gave me a way to influence my anxiety levels in any situation, which was a pretty big deal. I began to remind myself again and again that writing or speaking my thoughts almost always had a positive effect on my state. I was practicing a way to cope with my anxiety, *and* I was taking the extra step of reinforcing that my coping strategy was actually working. This was slowly but surely changing my internal narrative about my anxiety and the thoughts that came with it. I no longer felt trapped in an anxiety loop. I now had some power in the process.

Again, not the sole cure for my anxiety disorder, but it was a huge leap forward for me. I recognised that I had a say in things. I could take action to change the anxiety situation. This was the solid ground to stand on I had longed for. I had spent so long on what felt like an icy downward slope that, at last, being on level ground was a tremendous relief to me.

FIRST THINGS SECOND

We can't always know how we will
solve a problem or even if we will.

Remember when I decided to throw myself back into the middle of giant shopping centres because I thought that's what I should do? Remember how that backfired on me? As it turns out, I was on the right track but just missing the firm footing. Let me explain.

Having access to good information that taught me about what I was experiencing was the first bit of stability in my recovery that I could hold onto. It was a start. Developing the consistent habit of getting thoughts out of my head to bring down my anxiety level and learning that I had some power was like pouring concrete over that bit of solid ground. It strengthened the base. I could put all my weight on it and not sink. It gave me a jumping-off point for the rest of my recovery.

Up until this time, the primary impact of my journaling and 'fear expression' routine was on the background anxiety I experienced all day long. While in the past, my anxiety would simmer from the minute I opened my eyes, and the thoughts I would have all day long would turn up the heat until the anxiety would boil over into panic, again and again, being able to relate differently to those thoughts finally turned down the flame. As the simmer lessened, so too did the constant boiling over.

I had not specifically planned to do this, but it was working, so I thought, *I'll take it!* While I was thrilled that it was working in that area, I still wasn't addressing the panic triggered by specific places or situations. Like supermarkets. Or shopping centres. Or even driving towards those places. I had left some stones unturned, and it was time to address them.

When most people are confronted with a recurring panic attack problem that seriously impacts their lives, they will do what they can to address that panic first and foremost. In retrospect, I can see that I did try that. I just didn't do it in a terribly productive way. My attempt was misguided and ineffective mainly because I was under-informed back then and had no firm ground to stand on. In trying to address the 'biggest' problem first, I failed.

Now, months later, I was accidentally working on my general background anxiety first, before addressing the panic. But it was working.

I have heard so many doctors and community members speak about medication being used first to bring down high anxiety levels. This seems to boost the ability to engage in therapy. In my case, working on that background anxiety first did what the drugs might have done. This enabled me to go back and attempt the exposures again.

I realise that the way I did it is probably not a common approach and may have been a bit backwards, but sometimes being backwards can work.

You know, first things second.

WAIT ... I NEED TOOLS?

As everything was playing out, Elliot and I continued to spend quite a bit of time together. Our conversations about anxiety and mental health progressed, and he introduced me to the idea of an 'anxiety toolkit'. He asked me what tools I had to help me and what tools I was using. I had not really thought of what I was learning and applying in this way. His words were an eye-opener. Elliott explained that not everyone is the same and that each of us should have a somewhat organised and curated kit full of mental health tools that we could use when needed.

How had I missed this simple concept?

Elliot told me about how he sometimes used meditation and mindfulness. He explained that talking openly about his mental health was so beneficial for him, which led us to conversations about journaling and its many forms. Elliot taught me how he used belly-breathing techniques successfully in many instances to help him focus his attention and move through his panic attacks. We talked about exercise and how he learnt to love taking after-work walks to clear his mind and bring down his stress level. Like everything else he shared, he never preached or prescribed. He only suggested and shared his experiences.

The idea of an anxiety toolkit was such a helpful organising concept that informed much of my recovery going forward, but for some reason, I had never thought about it this way until we talked about it. This is just another example of the power of good friends and a strong support system (more on this later).

GETTING READY – PUTTING THE TOOLS IN PLACE

I knew that I had to start facing my panic attacks and going into those places that triggered them. Our 'toolkit chats' helped me get ready to do that.

I had been journaling (quite a bit!) already and collecting other tools here and there without really knowing what I was doing. Now I knew how to be more intentional and productive in the way I applied my knowledge and used the habits I had discovered and developed. The result was that I organically developed a real kit full of useful tools and techniques that combined the knowledge I had gained through reading and research with practical actions. I was now getting markedly better.

Here are a few of those tools that you might find useful:

Journaling: This was really the start of my toolkit. I just didn't know it when I started. Getting my anxious irrational thoughts out of my head and onto paper or out into the open air was so helpful for me as I embarked on getting well. It was the first thing that gave me a glimpse of power and some small measure of control. I continued to journal as I progressed, sometimes writing my thoughts and sometimes chatting about how I was feeling and the anxiety I was experiencing. My journaling was not always the same, but it was almost always helpful.

Mindfulness: I first learnt about mindfulness as I continued to research anxiety and recovery. I downloaded a mindfulness app to my phone and would use it during the day when I had to take my mini-breaks at work. Retreating outside or to the men's room and using my mindfulness app was my first exposure to this tool.

In my many conversations with Elliot, we often spoke about mindfulness, meditation, and other mental health tools. He suggested other ways I could incorporate mindfulness before bed to help me sleep better and showed me some basic meditation and mindfulness techniques that helped me continue to bring my overall anxiety level down.

Exercise: I learnt to really enjoy and look forward to my lunchtime walks at work. At first, I walked only with Elliot, then I carried forward this practice into my next job. To this day, I still find time mid-afternoon to go for a stroll at least a few times a week! I also started going to the gym every morning. Engaging in exercise to start my day gave my body and brain a much-needed one- to two-hour break from worry and rumination and everything that came with it. There is so much research and information that tells us that exercise is an excellent stress-management and mood-boosting tool. In my personal experience, this was absolutely true. Beyond just helping to lower my anxiety level and improve my mood, exercise became another way for me to learn that I had power in this process, that I was capable of facing my anxiety and moving towards recovery.

I should mention that my use of exercise as a recovery tool was not always smooth. The effects of exercise would occasionally be misinterpreted by my brain as anxiety or even panic. After ten minutes on a treadmill, my body would react in a way that would almost exactly mimic the sensations of panic. My heart would race. I would breathe hard and sweat.

Exercise—especially cardio—can create a response that looks and feels just like a panic attack. This is widely reported in the community, and I can confirm from first-hand experience that it really is a thing. If this is happening to you, take heart. Know that it is a very normal experience and does not indicate that you will be unable to recover.

If, while you're exercising, something truly doesn't feel right to you and you haven't been checked by a qualified health professional, stop exercising until you can get a doctor to sign off that you are healthy enough to do so.

Make sure you're healthy before you blame anxiety for your symptoms.

I was able to work through this natural response and meet the challenge using my 'observe and reframe' tools. It was scary and uncomfortable for sure, but I observed the striking similarities between how I felt during panic and how I felt during exercise. Then I could see that the exercise response was not only normal and expected but beneficial. You exercise to breathe hard, sweat, and elevate your heart rate. These are good things from a health perspective. Reframing the experience in this light helped me avoid going into escape-and-avoidance mode, and that allowed me to get more comfortable with these sensations over time. Cue the wonderful effect of making them seem far less scary and dangerous than they once were.

Are there 'feel good' endorphins involved with exercise? Sure. Did that help me? Probably. But the most important use for my 'exercise tool' was familiarising myself with panic sensations and desensitising myself to them.

This may seem like a pretty sparse recovery toolkit. I prefer to call it curated. Toolkits come in all shapes and sizes. These are the tools that I sharpened and worked with in my specific recovery situation. I made the conscious choice to try things, give them a chance for a while, then evaluate how they were working for me. It was pretty methodical. Learning that journaling, mindfulness, and exercise are three of the most popular anxiety-related mental health tools made them one of the first things I grabbed. Because I was getting good results from them, I felt that I could stick with them. I had no need to look in every corner for new tools to throw at my anxiety. I didn't try or use many other things simply because I did not feel a need or desire to do so. This was working for me, so I stuck with it.

The tools in your recovery kit may be the same, they may be different, or you may have a combination of both. That is perfectly okay.

Recovery does not look the same for everyone.

There is no one-size-fits-all anxiety toolkit that will universally catapult us towards recovery. I wish there was, but we all find what works for us in our own way, and that's just fine.

NO LONGER ADRIFT

When I reached my enough-is-enough point, I was in a very bad place. My world was shrinking. I felt weak, hopeless, and out of control. Anxiety dictated and controlled almost every aspect of every waking moment of my life. I was always afraid, always on guard, always trying desperately to keep panic at bay, and exhausted by it all. My mind was continually awash in anxious, scary, irrational thoughts that I felt powerless over. Alone, it seemed nobody else in the world could possibly understand my situation. Worst of all, I did not know what to do next.

Looking back, my state of desperation finally nudged me in the right direction. It forced me to go back to the doctor and start reading and learning. It forced me to take new actions—even when I had no faith that those actions would matter, or knowledge of how or if they might work.

Reaching the point where I was willing to try anything was not what I would have hoped for, but it was where I needed to wind up before my circumstances could improve for me. It doesn't make me happy to know that I had to reach such a low point to start enacting positive change, but I can accept that. It simply was the way it had to be.

Now I was pointed in the right direction. My overall anxiety levels were down. I had tools, skills, and power, and I was using them. As I was no longer afraid all the time, I was actually beginning to enjoy my work again. That meant I was being more productive too! More than anything else, my new approach meant that my simmering rarely, if ever, boiled over into panic. As a bonus, I wasn't really experiencing panic at work anymore. This gave me much less reason to wake up worried and dread the day.

Life was on an uptick, but I knew I had more work to do.

In the beginning of my anxiety journey, I had started adrift in a storm and gradually lost most of my hope. Now, the tide had truly turned.

It was time to tackle the final obstacles.

CHAPTER 6

TACKLING PANIC

It was the end of a working week in February of 2018, nineteen full months since my first panic attack. It had been a really good day and week for me. I'd felt my anxiety all day, but I wasn't really paying much attention to it. My anxiety level wasn't nearly as high as it used to be. My focus was on my work most of the time. I was becoming more organised and productive while feeling less overall anxiety. I was pretty excited about the whole process and the progress I was making.

I decided on this day that I would go back into the belly of the beast. I was going to return to the big shopping centre where I had attempted those first misguided exposures so long ago. I had experienced so many highly impactful panic attacks at that place, and they had started me down a slippery slope that shrunk my life day by day.

Returning to that place was—in my mind—the final hurdle, my last big challenge. It was time. I phoned my partner from work and told her that I wanted to go shopping after work. Then I set out in the direction of the shopping centre ...

Although I was apprehensive about revisiting
'the scene of the crime', I was also energised and ready.

On the drive to the shopping centre, I did not focus on how I felt. Instead, I focused on having a nice time shopping then going to a restaurant for an evening meal. I was nervous but excited. Ahead of me was a pastime that I used to love so much that anxiety had taken from me for far too long. I wanted it back. I wanted *all* of my life back.

IN THE BELLY OF THE BEAST

As we walked around the shops, the anxiety simmered inside me. It was with me. I was responding to the old conditioning that told me I was in a dangerous place. I knew enough by this time to expect the feeling. I didn't like it, but it was not a surprise and no longer a mystery. I understood why it was happening. I knew what I had to do. Nonetheless, it persisted.

I was in a large department store when I became aware of the anxiety beginning to rise. The feeling was unmistakable and oh so familiar. This is how it always felt when panic was on the hunt, stalking me. I had a feeling this would happen, and now it was. In the past, I would have stopped and focused intently on the feeling, but it was different now. I kept moving. I did my very best to remain focused on shopping. I browsed through the racks, picking up products, noticing them, focusing on them, all the while feeling the anxiety edge close to that boiling-over point.

My breathing was shallow. But that was okay. Knowing what I knew from all the research and learning I'd done, I was able to correct my breath. I went from rapid, gasping breathing to more intentional, regular breathing. I did not stop or leave the centre. My job was to remain engaged with the task of shopping and breathe the way I knew I had to.

At some point, I realised the rise of my creeping anxiety had stopped. The anxiety was still there in the background, but it was no longer heading towards a horrible crescendo. It was holding steady. Rather than moving towards panic, the anxiety settled back down into a normal place. Well, normal for me. That meant I still felt anxious, but it was manageable at a lower level. Sure, it was uncomfortable, but it didn't feel dangerous or like something that I had to watch. It just was. And so was I. Most importantly, I was okay.

RELEASE

After about fifteen minutes, a wave of emotion
came over me when I realised what I had done.

Still in the shop, I broke down at my accomplishment. I didn't care who saw me do it. All the work I had done before this moment came to fruition as I looked panic in the eye and stopped it from overwhelming me.

All the reading and researching, and learning.

All the wondering and doubting.

All the small steps that I had no confidence in while I was taking them.

All the conversations.

All the lunchtime walks.

All the journaling, breathing, and mindfulness practice.

All the exercise.

All the practice of moving through my days while anxiety sat next to me and badgered me.

It had all come to this. I had returned to the place that I feared most, and I came through the challenge with flying colours. It was too much. Such a release. I had been waiting for that moment for so long, and now I was living it. Joy, pride, accomplishment, gratitude, and probably fifteen other emotions flowed through me all at once. It was overwhelming. I could not control the tears streaming from my eyes. I will never forget that moment.

After leaving the shopping centre, my partner and I went to dinner at a restaurant where we sat and enjoyed a meal together. I don't know how she didn't get up and run because every three minutes, I repeated, in awe at myself, a huge smile on my face, 'I did it.' Sticking it out in that centre was unreal and unbelievable, but it had happened. I know shopping and eating at a restaurant hardly qualifies as a triumph for most people, but for me, that evening was everything. I might as well have won the Euro Cup, the World Cup, and an Olympic gold medal all at once. Sitting there at that table, enjoying my evening, basking in my achievement and what felt like a complete victory over the monster that had dragged me into a dark pit, was one of the most beautiful moments of my life.

NOT AFRAID OF BEING AFRAID

Before I get too carried away and give you the wrong impression, let me re-state I was not anxiety-free that evening.

Make no mistake. I was anxious.

I felt it in my bones. I felt it rising. It was coming to get me, but that almost didn't matter because I knew what to do. Anxiety was still present and asserting itself as it always had. So please don't think returning to the centre was a blissful, calm stroll through paradise. This was a challenge. It was quite difficult.

But ... I did not feel afraid of it. *That* was the difference.

That resolve to stay and be aware but not scared allowed me to keep going rather than freezing or fleeing. I did not banish my anxiety completely that night, but I did face and overcome my *fear of being anxious*. That is everything. It is where I want you to get to—existing side by side with your anxiety without letting it control you.

THE MOMENTUM BUILDS

No, I was not cured after one victorious trip to a shopping centre. My work was just beginning as I had to repeat returning to this triggering area as often as I could over the next 10–12 weeks.

Each time I made the trip, the outcome was the same. I would feel anxious but at a lower level, and my feelings would not accelerate into panic. It was unmistakable; I was getting better and better at moving past the feeling and staying focused on the task at hand. My confidence grew with each trip. I had cracked the panic code, and the monster couldn't catch me anymore.

The repeated trips to shopping centres to practice and cement my progress also had a positive effect at work and elsewhere in my day-to-day life. Learning to deal with the all-day anxiety at work helped me face the panic in my most-feared situations. In return, learning how to face my panic accelerated the progress in my day-to-day life.

My momentum and confidence grew and grew. I was no longer measuring my anxiety to see if it was rising. I stopped looking for panic.

'Will I panic today?'—a question I had asked myself repeatedly—no longer cropped up in my head.

But another question kept popping up over and over.
I wasn't sure how to answer it. Yet.

CHAPTER 7

ANXIETY RECOVERY

'Am I recovered from anxiety?'

I was visiting Elliot and sitting on his sofa—the sofa that had seen so many anxiety discussions over time. This question was the new puzzle I had to solve.

I wasn't feeling anxiety, stress, panic, or tension at work anymore. I was more productive than I had been in a very long time. I'd returned to the shopping centres and restaurants with steadily decreasing levels of anxiety and no sign of actual panic for the last few months.

So I asked my friend and mentor, 'Am I recovered from anxiety?'

He flipped the question right back at me.

'I don't know, Dean. Have you recovered from anxiety?'

His putting the answer on my shoulders made me really think about it. We started a great conversation about what anxiety recovery really looks like.

I did feel like I was recovered. My rationale was that even though I still felt anxious, I had no problem engaging in life again. I was working, hiking, socialising, shopping, driving, and doing everything I hadn't been able to do for so long. Anxiety was there at lower levels, but it was mostly a non-issue. It was not in control of my life any longer.

I spoke this out loud to Elliot, reasoning my way through the point. He thought for a second, then spoke.

> **'If you feel like you are recovered, then you are recovered.'**

I won't lie. This confused the hell out of me. I left his house that night, not sure what he really meant. When I arrived home, I went on a bit of a Google spree to dig into this topic. I'm happy to say that this time my Google searching was quite productive. It helped me gain a better understanding of my situation and how to interpret it. Even my Google habits had changed for the better.

What I discovered in my reading remains interesting to me to this day. As it turns out, the definition of recovery seems to vary from person to person. We all go through our own personal anxiety journeys that involve different combinations of symptoms and emotions and different combinations of triggers and life circumstances. When you recognise this, it makes sense that everyone has their own measuring stick when it comes to anxiety and recovery.

My measuring sticks were found in the shopping centres and in my workplace. Others may measure recovery based on what happens to them on the motorways, at family gatherings, or when left home alone. We share so much in common when it comes to our anxiety experience, but our recovery stories will vary—sometimes widely.

> **This made all kinds of sense to me, but at the same time, it triggered some old 'What if?' thinking.**

'I feel recovered, but what if I'm *not* recovered because I still feel anxiety when I'm sitting at my desk or walking through a shopping centre? What if there's still lots more work to do and I don't know that? What if it never gets better than this?'

This is where Elliot, who was such a recovery mentor for me, was so helpful. In our next conversation about the definition of recovery, he shared what recovery meant for him, acknowledging that recovery was different for different people. I learnt that he defined his recovery by his ability to do the things he had been putting off because of anxiety and fear. He did not worry that he still felt anxious sometimes but was more concerned with the fact that being anxious was just not terribly impactful in his life any more. It did not lead to restrictions, retreats, or avoidances any more. That was what defined his recovery.

He still experienced anxiety but felt fully recovered.

Can you imagine a world without anxiety? Life could get quite comfortable, but really hazardous for us, couldn't it? Anxiety serves a purpose. It warns us of real dangers and threats when they exist. Anxiety tells us to run back to the pavement when we see a car speeding in our direction. Anxiety tells us to avoid the dark alley alone at night. Anxiety puts us in a useful state of alert when it is warranted. It keeps us safe when we truly need it—and it has been doing this important job for human beings and our ancestors for millions of years. Anxiety serves a purpose. It *belongs* in human beings.

This is why we cannot expect that being recovered will mean that we never feel anxiety. That would be impractical and probably impossible. It would also likely be unsafe.

Many people will lament the loss of their old selves that 'never felt anxious'. I used to feel that way too. I wanted to go back to the old version of Dean that didn't have any anxiety. But that is misguided. We all have anxiety now and then. Even before the onset of my anxiety disorder, I most certainly did experience anxiety in various forms. I just didn't really think much about it because I understood that I felt that way for a reason. The anxiety itself did not represent a threat to me in my pre-disorder days.

When I was struggling, part of the struggle was based on the desire to become completely anxiety-free. I had totally discounted the fact that pre-disorder, I had experienced anxiety, but that I had done so without calling it a nightmare.

I wanted to be the old me again, but I was remembering an anxiety-free version of me that simply did not exist and *should not* exist.

When we are in a bad place, this can happen. We can lose perspective and aim at targets that we will never be able to hit.

Our emotional states can be made worse by the tidal wave of information and marketing on social media that will try to sell an anxiety-free state. For someone well on the road to recovery, this message can be confusing. It was for me. I saw so many advertisements for anxiety cures that promised I would be anxiety-free. That misleading message stuck with me, so when I did reach a recovered state, I doubted it! I didn't have to doubt it, but the concept of being without anxiety had been drilled into me. I had to do some work to get it out.

Elliot knew how to define his recovery. It was not based on never being anxious. He was open enough to tell me that he had experienced what most of us would call setbacks here and there. I felt like I needed to examine that a bit more so I could be better versed on setbacks and what they were.

In my (productive) research, I did learn that people who suffer through an anxiety disorder once are more likely than others to deal with anxiety disorders again. Interestingly, this fact does not frighten me. It actually gives me what I think is a helpful, realistic perspective.

Life can really be shit sometimes. We experience loss and grief and disappointment and betrayal and hurt—none of that is good. So we react to that and wind up immersed in a roiling pot of emotion at times. That's a normal reaction. Among those emotions might be anxiety; it might be the feeling that it can happen again. That's okay. I would rather have a realistic and productive view of life than expect some sort of magic to make me happy and anxiety-free all the time.

Losing my father is a great example of the watershed of emotions that overcame me because it sucked beyond description. I could not control that catastrophic loss. It triggered deep grief and a massive wave of other emotions, and it even kickstarted my anxious state. This happens sometimes. It might happen to me again.

TRIGGERS

All anxiety has a trigger or set of triggers. Life is a trigger. We are busy. We get stressed. We have to deal with challenges and upsets. Sometimes we are confronted by major life events that can lead to feeling anxious. One of the most important lessons I learnt in my recovery journey was that the triggers didn't really matter anymore, once I developed a true anxiety disorder.

When that happened, the anxiety itself became the trigger for more anxiety, and I spiralled out of control as a result.

What's critical in my recovery definition is that I now have the knowledge, understanding, and tools to handle it when life comes at me in a negative way. Certain events may trigger anxious moments for me, but I can't forget what I've learnt and the experiences I've had. They will stay with me. They will remain useful for me. They will inform my choices if I am confronted with anxiety again. My experience and knowledge mean I can go forward in confidence with my chest out and my chin up, not fearing anxiety if it were to appear again. Feeling anxious will never trigger extra anxiety for me ever again. Feeling anxious will simply be feeling anxious, and that's okay.

Elliot confirmed this fact with his own story of setbacks. Life events triggered setbacks for him from time to time, but he described being able to move through them faster and with less difficulty than he had in the past. What he had learnt and experienced mattered. He spoke of being so well-equipped to handle anxiety now that he had no worries about it and was not thinking about what role anxiety may or may not play in his future.

I was in a similar boat, as all the psychoeducation, exposures, practicing, and experiencing were additive for me. The more work I did in these areas, the more I confronted my anxiety, the easier it became to live with the prospect of anxiety, and the more confident I grew. At this stage, emboldened by my recovery, I went intentionally into the middle of the largest shopping centres, almost daring the anxiety to come and get me. If it did, I knew it would have no real impact. It was enjoyable to flex my new 'anxiety muscles'.

I saw this growing confidence at the barber's too. Getting my hair cut had been such a huge challenge for me when I was stuck in my anxiety disorder. I dreaded having to sit there trying to hold off the panic for what felt like hours. In that chair, I was trapped and vulnerable. The simple act of someone cutting my hair had turned into a nightmare. But once I had the hang of facing anxiety and handling it more productively and effectively, attending to this regular task became a non-issue for me.

But I was just getting started reclaiming my life. One moment in my recovery journey erased and finally eliminated any doubt I was not well.

On this particular day, I went to a different shopping centre, one I was not used to being in. The anxiety came. I assumed that I had it handled, but I was wrong. It quickly boiled over into panic. I had not experienced this out-of-control sensation in so long. It was surprising and initially very upsetting. I had all the usual symptoms. The racing heart.

The shallow breathing. The sweating. The derealisation. The intense desire to run to safety. It was all there again after so long, and right up in my face, breathing fire at me. This was the full monster unleashed, terrifying and shaking me to my core—like it always had.

Here is where the magic comes in.

Every other time I had experienced panic in a shopping centre, I would immediately exit the situation and seek comfort and safety in that exit. I would feel like running—so I would run and literally leave the premises.

Not this time.

Not.

This.

Time.

Even though I felt frightened, disorientated, and intense looming danger and doom, I did not leave. I continued to shop, moving through the space as slowly and as intently as I could. All the learning and practicing, and incorporating of my new tools came down to that moment. I was moving *through* a massive panic attack in a huge shopping centre. I was not running. Not anymore.

It felt really horrible for five or ten minutes, but then it was over, and I was standing at the top of the recovery mountain. I was shaken a bit. It took another little while for my body to completely come down, but I was absolutely elated. That was it. The final test. Panic. And I had passed it with flying colours.

At that moment, I knew anxiety in all its forms would never control me ever again. Background anxiety, rising anxiety, or full-blown panic could ambush me, but I could stand my ground without shrinking from it or being afraid. I had simply reached the point of not caring any more. It had no hold on me.

'Was I recovered from anxiety?'
This time, when I thought on that question,
only one word echoed in my head.
Yes.

CHAPTER 8

THE SCIENCE BEHIND WHAT WORKED FOR ME

Research and the evidence behind what worked for me in my recovery matters. I am not sharing this with you on the basis of what feels good or sounds good. Quite a number of smart, dedicated, and well-educated researchers and clinicians who have been conducting research into anxiety disorders and their treatment for decades can corroborate why the steps I took worked. We're learning more every day and compiling more and more evidence that supports the direction I chose to take in my recovery.

But I don't want you to take my word for all this.
I simply followed what I was learning and what
seems to be well supported in scientific literature.

Allow me to share that with you.

Understand as we talk about the science behind recovery that it is not absolute or unchanging. Science isn't really information or data. Science is a method. It's how we've agreed to test our theories about how things work, how we will pool our test results, and how we will try to come to a general consensus on 'truth'. The scientific method is fantastic, to be sure, but the method itself mandates that ideas are always open to a challenge. Questioning the status quo and advancing new ideas and theories is not only welcomed but encouraged and even required. We do not rest on our scientific laurels. We keep asking, probing, and testing. Theories can change and evolve over time and often do. Then we test more, examine more, and compile more data. Our conclusions grow richer and deeper over time.

It's important that we don't hold up science as truth set in stone forever. We can follow the research on any given day and make the best choices we can based on what we know on that day. That is how I used the available research in this field, how I continue to use it, and how I suggest you use it as well.

One last caveat before I go on. Please do not interpret this chapter as claiming that my way is the only way or the one true way. It takes a very long time for humans to arrive at a very wide consensus about what is the true way for anything. While research into the fields of anxiety disorders and recovery has given us so much in the last seventy years or so, we are nowhere near the point where research results are accepted in the same way as we all now accept that the earth orbits the sun. This process took a few thousand years to agree on, so we still have a way to go when it comes to the anxiety stuff.

My story and my journey are based on what I think was the best data available at the time. I would urge you to consider your choices using updated and relevant information when making your recovery choices. In the end, make those choices based on what is best for you.

CBT – COGNITIVE BEHAVIOURAL THERAPY

CBT looks at the relationship between your thoughts and your behaviour.

- What are you thinking?
- How are those thoughts making you feel?
- How are you behaving in relation to those thoughts and those feelings?

Remember my 11 a.m. witching hour? As you know, I used to think that 11 a.m. represented certain doom and the unavoidable onset of high anxiety and panic. As I did not want to experience those things, it made me afraid. This then drove my escape and avoidance rituals, such as excusing myself to the bathroom so I could calm down. In the moment, I was acting based on the conclusion that my anxiety would be too much for me to handle if I was sitting at my desk alongside my teammates. I was thinking. I was feeling. I was behaving in response to what my thoughts and feelings were telling me.

Let's break this down.

When I developed the habit of writing down my anxious thoughts, as 11 a.m. approached each day, I would record what popped into my head.

'11 a.m. is coming. Maybe this time, it will be even worse!'

'My heart is racing. Already. Am I sure I'm okay?'

'What if this time I can't cope?'

'If I get stuck on a call when the panic comes, I will be totally screwed.'

My psychoeducation research taught me that thoughts are not facts. Just because we think a thing does not make it true.

I would therefore begin to question and challenge my thoughts based on 'Accept, Reject, and Replace'.

For example, in response to the above thoughts, I would respond as follows.

'Yes, 11 a.m. is coming. This is true. Maybe the anxiety will be worse than it ever was. But maybe it will be less intense this time.'

'Yes, my heart is racing because I am afraid. My body is doing what it is supposed to do now. It will come down again when I am no longer afraid. I wasn't afraid last night and it wasn't beating very fast at all.'

'There is no evidence that I can see to support the idea that I can't cope with anxiety. I've been anxious, on edge, and hyper-aware of how I've felt, but I have always coped. Nothing bad ever actually happened. I will reject the thought that I can't cope.'

'If I'm stuck on a call when I'm anxious, then I'm just stuck on a call when I'm anxious. Anxious does not equal "screwed". I don't want to be anxious, but it's never been a disaster when I have become anxious. I've had so much practice being anxious and experiencing panic that the people around me rarely even know when it happens! There's no reason for me to accept or follow the thought that I will be somehow screwed, is there?'

Countering my irrational thoughts helped me hold them accountable for their nonsense. Challenging them based on my actual experience then replacing the imagined catastrophe with a more plausible outcome is called cognitive reframing. This would account for about 99 per cent of my journal entries.

It's important to note that I was not simply trying to think opposite, positive thoughts. That would be too far-fetched and unbelievable to an anxious brain.

Instead, I challenged myself to select more neutral and attainable outcomes. For example, when I would think that I would have a panic attack, I would reframe the thoughts that rushed at me with the thought that I had experienced many panic attacks. As a result, I had the tools to handle them, and I always did handle them. I would remind myself that there was no reason to believe this time would be any different. There was no forced insistence that panic would not happen or that I would be happy or peaceful. I kept my reframing realistic and neutral.

At the end of the day or the week, I did switch up my messaging a bit and added some positive thinking by making journal entries that recorded my victories—even when they were small. I tried to do one to three entries like this every day, covering what went well during the day; then I would summarise these triumphs at the end of the week. This helped me stay connected to my real progress and provided much-needed encouragement, motivation, and, yes— positivity.

MINDFULNESS. GROUNDING. PROPER BREATHING

What did I do when anxiety did boil over and become panic?

In those moments when anxiety felt like it was running rampant again, mindfulness, grounding, and proper breathing came into play. Being mindful helped me separate myself from racing, irrational thoughts after being gripped by them for so long.

When I did that, I could finally see that my thoughts were not the source of my anxiety. No, my behaviour was. Coming to that realisation was powerful.

We often fall into the trap of trying to get rid of anxious thoughts— especially when anxiety first rears its ugly head. When we realise that our thoughts can be anything and that how we react to them, behave towards them, and give them our attention fuels the anxiety, that can be a magic moment.

Consider two friends out for a cup of coffee, then returning to work on the third floor of their office building. Both are wearing a fitness watch. Both finish their coffee, walk up three flights of stairs, then notice that the gadget on their wrist reads 130 beats per minute. Both take note of this high heart rate.

'Hey, my heart is really beating.' This is the common thought. But the reactions to that thought can be very different.

The anxious friend will think about being triggered into panic by caffeine. They will worry about the outcomes associated with panic.

Losing control.

Not coping.

Becoming incapacitated.

These thoughts will fill them with dread, supercharging fear, and the fear response. Their heart will continue to race accordingly, causing them to focus even more intently on the number they see on the watch face. This will create more fear and anxiety and drive them into a panic state where they desperately try to calm down and escape. This feeling will persist until all the adrenaline and cortisol has been used up, at which point the anxious friend will wind up completely knackered and want to go and lie down for the rest of the day.

Conversely, the non-anxious friend will respond to 'Hey, my heart is really beating' in a totally different way. They will recognise that climbing three flights of stairs will cause a rapid heartbeat. They will remember they've also just had coffee, which contributes to a higher heart rate. They will see no threat and no dire outcome associated with thinking about this elevation. The non-anxious friend will return to work without skipping a beat from acknowledging their thoughts to setting to the tasks at hand. Their heartbeat will slow down and return to its base level. It's a non-event for them in every sense of the word.

**Same thought. Different reactions. Different behaviours.
Completely different outcomes.**

What does this teach us?

Learning to be mindful, and to pay attention with intention and without judgement is what led me down the path to recognising the relationship between my behaviours and reactions and my anxiety levels. The ability to create space between thought and reaction allowed me to see this clearly.

When I was delving into mindfulness and learning the practice, I found the Headspace app quite useful. It offered calming voices and clear explanations of the process of anxiety. Going through the mindfulness, grounding, and breathing exercises was very helpful for me.

The app taught me that most of us breathe incorrectly. We focus on our chests rather than our diaphragms. I learnt to recognise that one of the signals of an anxiety build-up was the increasing shallowness of my breath. I used the breathing exercises to interrupt this process when I was feeling it and return myself to a better breathing rhythm. I would even occasionally use my fitness watch to observe how my heart would slow down while I was doing my breathing exercises.

Some may say that this use of my watch was a bit of a crutch or a safety behaviour. Maybe. Did it matter for me? Not at all.

Remember when I said that we all make our own choices and find what works for us? This is a perfect illustration of that.

Scan the QR code to watch a short introduction to mindfulness video

EXPOSURE AND EXPOSURE THERAPY. MY 'PANIC KIT'.

Ideally, exposure therapy is done under the guidance of a therapist or counsellor, but many people do this on their own. I was one of them.

There is quite a large body of evidence that tells us that exposure work is highly effective in the treatment of anxiety disorders. Interestingly, there is also a rather large number of therapists who shy away from using exposure, even in the face of this evidence. This seems to be based on a worry that intentionally making a client feel 'bad' might be harmful or unethical in some way.

I only bring up these polarising views to illustrate that it can be difficult to find a therapist who will work with you on doing exposure work to treat your anxiety disorder. This is why it's super important to ask questions to find the right therapist who works for you. If exposure therapy is something you want to try with a therapist, ask them if they will be comfortable guiding you through it. If they don't feel comfortable, it's perfectly okay to search for a new therapist who does feel comfortable. Therapy is a two-way street.

If I had gone to a therapist, it's possible that I would have never gone down the path of exposure work. But I did not engage a therapist, and exposure was the path I decided to take in my recovery.

As I was doing my research, I continually unearthed information that referenced the benefits and effectiveness of exposure therapy. Even after stumbling over my first attempt at what I thought was exposure in that shopping centre, what I was reading gave me the confidence to try again. My first experience was not so good, but I still believed that it would work for me based on what I was learning.

This is a good rule of thumb to remember:
you will not nail recovery the first time you try exposure.
That's not the point. What matters is that you keep trying.

You don't have to be perfect for it to eventually work—and you won't be.

Exposure therapy is based on the idea that putting yourself into situations you fear gives you a chance to learn through new experiences that those situations are actually not dangerous at all. The idea is to allow fear and even panic, move through it, and come out the other side without actual harm or damage done to you. This experience provides us with the evidence we need to change our view of those 'scary' situations and the 'dangers' of anxiety and panic. That evidence helps us no longer fear our symptoms and sensations. It teaches us that left to its own devices without fighting or trying to escape it, panic will always subside. We will always return to our base level. Exposure gives us the opportunity to practice moving through panic and anxiety so that we can become more confident in our ability to cope when it strikes.

When done repeatedly, exposure therapy teaches our brains that interpreting anxiety, panic, and specific places or situations as dangerous is wrong and no longer required in situations where we are safe. Exposure repetition leads to a gradual decrease in the intensity and duration of each anxious episode, which in turn leads to a decrease in the frequency of anxious episodes and panic attacks overall. It has been shown again and again by repeated research to be very effective.

Exposure worked exactly as advertised for me once I understood how to engage in it. It did decrease my anxiety level over time. It also decreased the duration of anxiety spikes when they did happen, and it ultimately led to no longer being afraid to go into shopping centres. What exposure really taught me was that even if I do get anxious in a given situation, I can always handle it.

With this new knowledge, I simply do not see anxiety and panic as dangerous or horrible any longer.

Unpleasant?

Absolutely!

Desired?

No way.

Again, that doesn't matter. I do not have to let it dictate my choices or control my life—that's what matters. That was the turning point I wanted.

I may have a panic attack in a shopping centre tomorrow. It just doesn't matter to me if I do. Thank you, exposure!

EXERCISE

Exercise was very beneficial for me in the mornings before work. Most mornings, I would go to the gym for a cardio session or a swim. This would boost my energy levels for work while also reducing my morning anxiety. It would clear my anxious thoughts so I could start the day level-headed and clear-minded. If you look for information about ways to effectively address anxiety, exercise is going to pop up again and again. There's a reason for that.[1]

MEDITATION FOR IMPROVED SLEEP

As I used mindfulness practices throughout the day, I learnt that meditation was an important tool in learning to be mindful. Meditation has so many benefits when it comes to reducing anxiety and overall stress levels. I wanted to find a spot in my day where I could practice meditation on a regular basis. Since I was reading about all this goodness, I wanted some of it!

In my research, I found a bunch of guided meditation videos and recordings online, then stumbled upon one for sleep.

Perfect! While I wasn't overly anxious at bedtime, safe in my home, I am a natural night owl and always have been. I find it hard to wind down, let go, and get to sleep. I would often lie in bed with my mind racing through all kinds of thoughts and ideas. I was hopeful that meditation might help me quiet my mind so I would have an easier time getting to sleep and staying asleep.

My new practice was getting into bed, putting on my headphones, and listening to a guided meditation called 'body scanning'. It taught me to bring my attention to the position of my body in the moment. I could

---

[1] https://bmchealthservres.biomedcentral.com/articles/10.1186/s12913-018-3313-5

feel how it was contacting the surface I was lying on. When I was scanning, I would start at my feet then work all the way up to my head. The video instructed me to bring my focus back to specific parts of my body whenever my mind wandered off. It taught me to pay attention to my breathing and helped me recognise when I had thoughts that needed decelerating.

This focus and attention exercise just happened to use my body as a focal point. It worked quite well, calmed me down, put me in a relaxed state, and allowed me to let go of all the chatter in my head.

It worked so well that I would often find myself waking up in the morning with my headphones still on and a random YouTube video playing on my phone. I had fallen asleep even before the meditation had finished. Just what the doctor ordered.

I added this nightly practice into my routine straight away. It was yet another helpful tool in my kit that moved me down the road in my recovery. To this day, I still use it at least a few times every week.

Scan the QR code to watch a short introduction to meditation video

THANK YOU, SCIENCE!

Learning about CBT, mindfulness, exposure, and meditation were truly vital in my recovery journey. But learning about them only mattered because the evidence told me that they were likely to be helpful. I was certainly happy to hear the opinions of people who wanted to help me but utilising these tools comprised more than opinions. Knowing that these methods had been studied and mostly validated scientifically gave me confidence in them. It motivated me to try them, to stick with them even when they posed challenges, and ultimately to recognise that they really were giving me a positive impact every day.

I am a fan of science, and I am eternally grateful
for all the studies, experiments, and other
research that created the data I hang my hat on.

You may be a fan of science like I am. You may not pay it much mind. But when we understand it and use it well, it can give us a leg up in what can be a very challenging undertaking. I don't know about you, but I will take all the help I can.

Note: To learn more about the topics included in this chapter, including links to relevant research and other resources, please visit the "Resources" chapter at the end of this book.

CHAPTER 9

THE IMPORTANCE OF A SUPPORT NETWORK

Nobody should have to carry the burden
of an anxiety disorder alone.

Having a strong support network was vital in my recovery. Everyone should have one in place, no matter how large or small. You don't have to have 100 friends. Even one friend you can open up with and lean on can make a huge difference.

A support network can also consist of more than just friends and family. Your managers at work can be part of your support network. Your neighbours can be part of your support network. Teachers at school can be part of your support network. Faith leaders, mentors, and anyone you consider a trusted adviser can be part of your support network too. Depending on your situation, you may reveal more or less of your struggle to different people in your network. Even if you feel like your sharing is a bit fragmented, when you put it all together, it can add up to the relief, cheerleading, kindness, and practical life help that you need to get you through the rough times.

In many ways, I stumbled onto the different fragments of what would become my anxiety support network. I wasn't intentionally trying to assemble a multifaceted group of helpers and supporters. It all happened a bit accidentally and somewhat organically without intent. In the end, it worked out exactly as I needed it to, and I am grateful for that.

MY PARTNER

The first piece of my support network puzzle was my partner. I was open and 100 per cent honest with her right from the start of my anxiety journey. She knew everything and was completely supportive from day one. Sometimes we would sit together and read CBT articles and websites online. She helped me find helpful information when I needed it. Having her by my side really made me feel validated and supported. When she participated with me in the recovery research, it helped me to feel less like I was grasping at straws and more like I was being productive. And I *was* being productive, but on my worst days, my anxious brain couldn't be sure of that. My amazing partner helped keep me focused on the positive benefits of what I was doing.

She was also my rock when we were out and about. This was crucial. She always noticed when I was struggling and could sense my need to hear something encouraging in those moments. Having her tell me that I was okay and that she knew I could handle how I was feeling was empowering to me in what felt like my weakest moments. As I progressed in my recovery and learnt more and more about what was working and what to avoid, my partner was excellent at adapting how she spoke to me. She remained incredibly supportive while also steering clear of excessive reassurance and coddling. I could not have asked for more.

Is it possible that my partner was a bit of a crutch for me at times? Maybe, especially in the early days, but having her there when I was completely overwhelmed and feeling broken and out of control helped me get my feet under me again. This made it easier for me to take my first tiny steps forward.

MY MATE AND RECOVERY MENTOR

One of the most vital components of my support team came totally out of the blue the day Elliot called me into the staff room and shared his own mental health struggles with me. When he offered to be an ear for me and share his experience and knowledge, he handed me one of the main keys to my eventual recovery, maybe without even knowing he was doing it.

Since Elliot had already walked the path I was on, he could share his experiences in a highly relatable way. This was so helpful. He never hesitated to share details with me. Each time he did, it helped prop me up even more. Knowing that he had gone through exactly what I was going through helped build my confidence and belief that I could follow the path he did. He instilled in me that my recovery was possible.

Elliot was always there on the phone or on the other side of a text message when I had questions, felt lost, or just wanted to tell someone that I was struggling. He made himself available to me and never made me feel like I was intruding, overstepping, or bothering him in any way. His advice was so practical. He never tried to give me a miracle cure or offer false hope. Instead, he spoke to me honestly about what worked, what didn't, and further options I might want to consider. Hearing that he was just a 'regular guy' and that 'if I can recover, so can you' was precisely what I needed to hear on many days.

When I look back at the role he played, I also appreciate how calm Elliot was when I needed a calm voice. He knew all the tricks of anxiety, so he never fed into my fear or fanned those flames. He always responded to my anxious state with calmness and quiet confidence. When you feel like you are hanging on for dear life and about to fall apart, a soothing presence that shows you that everything is truly okay means more than you can imagine.

Having Elliot in my life as a friend and mentor played a huge role in moving me forward.

He helped get me ready to tackle the big exposures and the massive situational panic attacks that I still had not faced. He taught me. He inspired me. He propped me up when I needed it. He dropped useful breadcrumbs that I could follow as I found my way towards recovery.

I am forever grateful for the friendship, support, and encouragement Elliot gave me in the days when I needed it most. His support taught me that being alone was no way to deal with my mental health. It was Elliot who gave me my first glimpse of the power of community—even on a small scale.

I had no idea what that community would become one day.

MY GROUP OF FRIENDS

Then there were my other friends. I took a bit of a risk when I started telling them when I was feeling anxious or afraid. They could have looked at me funny and judged me harshly, but they didn't. They listened. They were kind and always supportive of me. I know most of them really didn't understand what I was describing, but that didn't matter. They still gave me space, rallied around me, and even pushed me a little when I needed it. Having the ability to open up to them was helpful. An anxiety disorder is hard enough to handle without also carrying the burden of trying to hide it. Being able to show myself completely, with my fear and every-thing, significantly relieved that pressure.

MY WORKPLACE FRIENDS AND TEAMMATES

The initial 'Let's keep this a secret' incident aside, my managers and teammates were very accepting of my situation. This gave me room to excuse myself for a few minutes if needed. It kept my work performance and interactions in the proper context. Nobody had to guess or wonder why I may have had a few stretches where I wasn't performing at my best. I didn't have to worry about being misunderstood, misinterpreted, or possibly dismissed from my position. That was another huge burden lifted off my shoulders.

I've heard unfortunate stories of job losses and economic hardship, all based on trying to hide anxiety issues from colleagues and managers. When hidden or denied, the change in performance that may occur can be misinterpreted as a lack of effort or irresponsibility. If possible, be open and honest with the people in your workplace. They can become an important part of your support network like mine was for me.

LOCAL MENTAL HEALTH SUPPORT GROUPS

On one trip to see my grief counsellor, I noticed a flyer on the wall in the waiting room announcing a local grief support group. I never attended a meeting of that group, but the fact that it existed stuck with me. I had not considered that type of resource before, probably because I never had to. Up until I developed an anxiety disorder, I had never experienced mental health issues that would have required that kind of support. Seeing people reaching out to each other in the local community showed me the value of community support even among people who are relative strangers to each other.

> That flyer planted some seeds that would
> ultimately grow into something amazing,
> but I had no idea that this was to come at the time.

ONLINE SUPPORT

We all live heavily digital lives now. We spend hours on end scrolling, reading, and consuming. The devices in our hands all the time can be troublesome, but they can also be gateways to other avenues of support. Creating or joining an online community of like-minded people who understand and share your struggle can give you an entire world of valuable support that was simply not available twenty years ago. Most of us love to complain about the internet and social media but used productively, the digital world can deliver vital support for anyone struggling with mental health issues.

**This was a lesson that I would take to heart in a big way.
Then I would act on it—in a BIG way.**

More on that in a moment.

WHEN PEOPLE DON'T UNDERSTAND

Before I share with you the incredible journey I've been on in helping to build an irreplaceable mental health network, I wanted to include a brief section of the types of interactions you don't want. Understand, even if you get a less-than-desired reception, it does not mean that you and what you are doing is not important. Sadly, as we move along a path to recovery, we may find that not everyone will be supportive or understanding. There are people in the world, and maybe even in your life, who might be dismissive of your struggle. They may see you as weak or broken. They may show little to no understanding of what you are going through. It should not be that way, but sometimes it is, so we have to acknowledge it.

When we run into these people, we must set healthy boundaries with them. We can offer to educate them and send them to online resources like the DLC Anxiety platform. We can do everything in our power to help them learn and understand, but if they are not receptive, then we must draw a line and back away. This can be especially difficult if these are people close to us, but it is important that we do not let the anger or ignorance of others derail us.

It's 2022. We should not have to defend ourselves against stigma and attack when it comes to our mental health, but sometimes we do.

Although the stigma appears to be less rigid and there are more resources available as well as learnings, we still have a long way to go. I am doing what I can to help to advance this cause. It has turned from a curiosity to help myself to a passion to help others.

Just how am I doing that?

Turn the page, and I'll tell you.

CHAPTER 10

BIRTH OF THE DLC
ANXIETY PLATFORM

Back on the Sofa of Destiny

When I look back at my anxiety journey and what has come out of it, I am surprised at one thing. The tremendous role Elliot's sofa played in shaping my life.

One day, post-panic disorder, I was back at Elliot's house, sitting on his sofa. That sofa had seen so many anxiety and mental health chats. It had been the staging ground for so much of my recovery and forward progress. On this day, unbeknownst to me, it was to become the launchpad for the DLC Anxiety mental health platform. I had simply gone to visit my mate to share some food and watch a film.

I had no idea how my life was about to change.

As we were eating and chatting, I asked Elliot, 'How can I bottle up the feeling you gave me when I was struggling? I want to capture the courage and motivation that you gave me in our talks. You made me feel less alone. You showed me that I was not isolated. You held up a torch for me and showed me the way when it was desperately needed. How can I do that for other people like you did for me?'

As I sat there, sharing a meal with Elliot, I was brimming with gratitude for his friendship and support. Beyond that, I felt driven to pay it forward. If I could, I would have put what he did into a bottle, sent it off to a factory, mass produced it, and got it into the hands of as many people as possible.

As the wheels turned in my head about what to do, I couldn't forget the flyer I saw in the waiting room at my counsellor's office. A local grief and loss support group seemed like such an incredible idea. I was inspired to see that people living through painful loss were willing to come together to share their experiences to help others. That was so wonderful. While I sometimes kicked myself for never having attended a meeting of that group when I needed it, I was totally enamoured with the idea that the group represented.

In these groups, I knew that people openly and freely shared experiences and stories to help others. I wanted to do that too, but on a larger scale.

The idea of what I could build burned inside me.

I was so enthusiastic that I even went so far as to ask my mate, 'How can I do this on the *biggest* scale possible? How can I create the largest and most useful community resource?'

Elliot and I kicked around ideas, including creating larger community support groups modelled after the grief group that had inspired me. But it didn't seem large enough. Local groups are great, and larger local groups are even better; however, I wanted to bring to life a truly global community that would be fully open to anyone who needed help.

Naturally, the internet came into play as I worked to define my vision. I poked around on Facebook, and I was encouraged when I found many groups that focused on mental health and wellness issues. That was a good sign, and Facebook is certainly a global platform, so I gave it some thought.

I asked myself *how can I use Facebook to build a platform to take anxiety support and mentorship and amplify it?*

My idea to explore this sort of group was promising, but what wasn't was that most of the groups were closed or private—they were not readily open to everyone. I also took note of the almost random way that people found those groups. There was good stuff on Facebook, but the place is just so huge that it's like wandering through a theme park the size of Scotland and hoping to stumble upon the one ride you love the most. The discovery process was random and chaotic. That really didn't sit too well with me. I would have to improve that for the future members.

ENTER, INSTAGRAM

My next stop was Instagram. I searched for 'anxiety', and found maybe four or five Instagram accounts focused on anxiety. It wasn't much, but those people were sharing their anxiety experiences, and I didn't have to join anything to see what they were doing. It was already there on the app.

I thought back to how it felt when I was Googling and trying to do my own research to find ways to help myself. I needed easy access back then. I didn't need barriers. I didn't want to join anything new. If I had searched for 'anxiety' on Instagram back then, it would have been very simple for me to navigate the results and get good content, especially when I was struggling and needed something I could put into play immediately.

Instagram seemed like the place. It was free, user-friendly, and finding anxiety information was fast and uncomplicated. I was sold. This was where I would plant the flag and get to work.

I turned to Elliot and said matter-of-factly, 'I am going to start here.'

I was so excited. Taking my anxiety support idea to Instagram would let me pay forward the help Elliot had given me when I so desperately needed it. I wanted to encourage the creation of as large a community as possible, but I also felt that as long as I could share my experiences openly to help even one person, then my mission would be accomplished. Elliot helped me. I could help someone else. That's what it was all about.

If I did it right, maybe this thing could help thousands of 'someone elses', which would be incredibly rewarding for everyone involved.

THE DLC ANXIETY JOURNEY BEGINS

Through the creation of my page on Instagram, I began to share my experiences. The symptoms I experienced. The struggles I endured. The lessons I had learnt. I just told my stories as openly as I could. I wasn't sure where it was going, but the sharing alone was very gratifying and I wanted to keep at it. For the next three to six months, I started attracting attention. The community grew steadily. I regularly got beautiful messages of thanks. In sharing my story and experience, I offered hope and encouragement to others going through what I had gone through.

These people were kind enough to express their gratitude for what I was doing. That motivated me to continue on. I had set out to help others as Elliot had helped me, and I was doing it. It felt so good. The more positive feedback I received, the more dedicated I became to the task.

As I got deeper into Instagram, I discovered some fantastic artists who were using their talent to address mental health issues. These awesome creators shared specific anxiety and mental health information and experiences in such a visually appealing way. They had found a way to combine the image-orientated nature of Instagram with a topic they clearly cared deeply about. I was inspired!

So I started sharing that artwork alongside my own information, sometimes putting my own spin on it in my captions. I also started sharing as much good information on the science of anxiety and recovery as I could. The number of contributors to the community increased. As we grew, I kept the doors open to any and all helpful content and spent a considerable amount of time seeking it out.

The DLC community was, from its inception, open to everyone. Any experience was welcomed. I was happy to shed light on any recovery methods that were working for people.

As more and more people shared what was working for them, the platform diversified. Some people shared about medication. Others about CBT. Still others would sing the praises of exercise as a recovery tool. I was happy to take it all in. If a member of the community was seeing success and wanted others to benefit from it, DLC was all ears.

From the very start, I wanted to create a community where everyone would feel welcome and validated.

My anxiety tool may have looked a certain way, but my experience was not necessarily universal or applicable to everyone. We're all different in so many ways. Knowing this, I was happy to get everything out into the open and on the table for discussion, regardless of whether it matched my experience or not.

This expansion of the content I shared drove more and more growth. As the community grew, so did the fabulous feedback I received from people who were consuming the content we were generating together.

When you wake up in the morning to messages of thanks and gratitude, that makes for a rosy start to any day. When another human being tells you that you've contributed to saving their life, you can't help but feel motivated to help even more. It was starting to feel like my struggles had all happened for a reason.

> The DLC community was making a difference in people's lives.
> It was tremendously rewarding work and still is.

VOICES AMPLIFY VOICES

At one point, the community had reached 150,000 followers on Instagram. I never imagined it would get this large. When that happens, the algorithm kicks in. Your content becomes visible to a wider audience beyond just your followers. The Instagram 'discover page' became my friend. The bigger the community got, the more attention it attracted from worldwide mental health professionals, mental health advocates, and celebrities speaking openly about mental health.

This meant there were relatively famous people finding posts from DLC Anxiety who then went on to share them with others. People with much larger audiences and much greater reach than I had were engaging with me. Their voices amplified the DLC community voice. When they found our information useful, they would tell people—often many people. That increased our reach beyond what I already considered a bit mind-bending.

Each day I would discover that more people at various levels of real-life and social media fame were picking up DLC content, finding it useful in their own struggles, and sharing it. When it comes to social media algorithms, the domino effect is real, and I was experiencing it.

The DLC community was picking up steam, and every day, getting larger and larger.

One of the reasons that we gained such momentum was Madison Beer. Madison came across my content at a time when she already had millions upon millions of people in her Instagram community. She was sharing openly about mental health in her Instagram stories. I always admire people who use their fame to help break the stigma and to help others know that they are not alone. As part of that effort, Madison began regularly sharing posts from DLC that struck a chord with her. Our community resonated with her, and she passed our message on to her millions of fans.

Her shares had a tremendous impact on the growth of the DLC Anxiety community. We quickly went from 150,000 followers to over 500,000 followers in what seemed like the blink of an eye. And it wasn't just Madison. Alessia Cara and others also shared our work and sent their audience to DLC Anxiety. I will forever be grateful to each of these people for the support they provided.

CONNECTING WITH MENTAL HEALTH PROFESSIONALS

As the community grew, it attracted some big names in the mental health world. Bestselling authors, doctors, and therapists like Dr Daniel Amen became regular supporters. They frequently shared our stories and the art and science content we posted about.

I absolutely loved making those connections. It felt like we were all coming together in the name of helping anyone in the Instagram community who was struggling with anxiety and other mental health issues. I found that so fulfilling. I still do! It motivated me, even more, to keep growing, improving, and making the DLC Anxiety platform as useful as it could be to as many people as possible.

Even more remarkable was the diversity in the overall DLC messaging that allowed us to discuss a wide range of important topics with a wide range of mental health professionals. Hearing so many varied points of view from so many well-educated and experienced professionals helped the community build a strong science and evidence-based backbone to support the overall discussion.

CHANGING FOCUS

As the platform grew, it was time to shift focus. I had set out to use my story and experience as a way to help others. I think I succeeded in that mission. But the community had grown far beyond just my story. It was much larger than me, and that made me happy.

DLC Anxiety was now a tool that could leverage
and amplify the stories and knowledge of many others.
It had truly become a vibrant community full of amazing
voices and diverse mental health experiences.

One day I stumbled quite accidentally upon a post by Dax, a musician who had just released a song called 'Joker'. The song was about anxiety, depression, and cyberbullying. Dax shared openly about his experiences. He was vulnerable in front of his audience and in front of the whole world. I not only loved his song but wanted to know what brought him to write it and share it that way.

Without hesitation, I reached out to Dax and invited him to do an Instagram Live with me. I explained that I loved his song, was touched by his willingness to share, and that I was hoping he would come on to talk to my community about what he was going through. My goal was simple: just tell the community what prompted him to write 'Joker' and share it with the world.

I composed my message,
hit the Send button, then waited.

CHAPTER 11

MENTAL HEALTH INTERVIEWS AND THE EVOLUTION OF THE PLATFORM

I didn't have to wait very long.

Dax responded quickly to my request. We did an Instagram Live interview within a few hours of my contact. He was so accommodating and helpful. I will always be thankful to Dax for being the first DLC Anxiety mental health interview. He helped get the ball rolling on a new feature of the platform.

This first interview was incredibly moving.

Dax was so open and willing to talk about his experience with cyberbullying. As Dax grew as an artist and in popularity, he encountered more people online who wanted to take him down. He became the subject of repetitive attacks from them, which is, of course, troublesome for many people. This was impactful for him, and he knew it was having a serious effect on many others. When I reached out, he decided he wanted to share his experience and address that issue through his art. That's why he wrote 'Joker' and shared it with the world. It's such a good story.

We didn't stop there. We talked about how Dax took care of his mental health in general. We went over what was working for him and what tools he was using to care for himself mentally and emotionally. Mindfulness, breathing exercises, and ways to get grounded were all things that Dax touched on in the interview as being beneficial to him in managing stress, anxiety, and his overall mood.

I was particularly interested in Dax's red light/green light strategy. He almost 'gamified' the process of recognising 'red light' thoughts and moods, working through them productively, and emerging into 'green light' territory. As he improved his mental health and self-care skills, he found he could go from a red light to a green light more quickly.

We also talked about how setting goals and adding structure was a positive thing for Dax and his mental health. He shared his experiences of anxiety and depression. We touched on how they appeared in his life as a performer. Getting naturally nervous or anxious before performing was a normal thing for Dax, so we talked about what that looked like and how he was handling it.

In the end, it was a fantastic hour spent conducting my first ever live interview. Being able to chat openly about mental health with someone not necessarily in the mental health community but certainly impacted by the issue offered a new perspective and a new dimension. Hearing from therapists and doctors is amazing. Watching a real person apply that information and the techniques we learn about is another stratosphere of amazing.

The Dax interview represented an 'evolution point' for the DLC Anxiety platform. I will remember it fondly forever.

The feedback on the Dax interview was overwhelmingly positive. So many lovely comments and DMs from the community about how helpful the session was poured in. People loved being able to ask questions and get immediate feedback. I knew immediately that I needed to conduct more interviews.

Scan the QR code to watch Dax's song, "Joker"

Scan the QR code to watch the DLC interview with Dax

DR SHAUNA SHAPIRO ON MINDFULNESS

From there, I spoke to Dr Shauna Shapiro, an expert in mindfulness, who shared thirty minutes chock-full of solid and practical information with the community. Dr Shapiro provided us with so many gems in that interview. I remember them all so clearly:

'The most valuable thing in the Universe is not time. It is attention. What we focus our attention on is the most important thing.'

'Be mindful with compassion and kindness. The important thing is the intention, not the result.'

'What you practice makes you grow stronger.'

'Mindfulness means to see clearly with compassion and kindness.'

Scan the QR code to watch the
DLC interview with Dr. Shauna Shapiro

DR RADHA ON ANXIETY SYMPTOMS

Dr Radha, the medical expert for BBC Radio 1's daytime show, *Life Hacks*, was my next interview. She was kind enough to spend time with the community to give her perspective as a medical doctor and the physical implications of anxiety and panic, as well as why specific therapies work on a physiological level. Of note in that interview was the understanding that most new anxiety sufferers, based on their physical symptoms of anxiety, seek out a medical doctor. We spoke about what role an MD can play in the anxiety journey, again providing well-grounded and practical advice and information for the DLC community.

Scan the QR code to watch the DLC interview with Dr. Radha

From there, the DLC interview series picked up steam. I spoke on a regular basis with prominent social media psychologists, therapists, and mental health advocates. I was also fortunate enough to interview social media celebrities who shared openly about their mental health. With each new interview, praise and positive feedback from the community grew. I had suspected these interviews would have a positive impact. The overwhelming show of support from the community confirmed that for me.

LILY CORNELL SILVER ON LOSS AND GEN-Z MENTAL HEALTH

My interview with mental health advocate Lily Cornell Silver generated a huge amount of positive feedback and praise for Lily and her willingness to speak freely about her own loss and mental health struggles. Lily spoke about the death of her father (Soundgarden lead vocalist Chris Cornell), how that impacted her mental health, and what tools she's put in place to cope with her anxiety and depression.

Lily advocated for the need to speak up and share feelings and experiences as part of the mental health journey. She spoke about her strong connection with friends and family and how important it is for her to share her experiences and feelings with them. We also touched on some of the unique mental health challenges faced by members of Generation Z. Those issues are real, and Lily did a fantastic job of addressing them in a meaningful interview.

Scan the QR code to see the DLC interview with Lily Cornell-Silver

DR DANIEL AMEN ON BRAIN HEALTH

It was a major win for the DLC Anxiety community when I got the chance to do my first interview with 12-time *New York Times* bestselling author Dr Daniel Amen. As a psychiatrist, Dr Amen is known as 'The Brain Doctor'. His voice is heard around the world advocating and educating on the topic of mental health, specifically focused on brain health. Dr Amen hates the term 'mental illness', preferring to focus more on brain health and taking a proactive approach to caring for your brain.

We spoke about the role of nutrition in promoting good brain health. Dr Amen shared his views on the negative impacts that society has on our emotional and mental well-being. The interview was jam-packed with words of wisdom and experience from a recognised leader and virtual legend in the mental health community.

Scan the QR code to watch the DLC interview with Dr. Amen

ALESSIA CARA ON MENTAL HEALTH AND THE MUSIC INDUSTRY

Music industry sensation Alessia Cara did a terrific job discussing the need to break the stigma surrounding mental health. Alessia revealed her struggles with anxiety and depression and highlighted the tools she's put in place to help her navigate those rough waters. We spoke about challenging irrational thoughts, using grounding and breathing techniques, and not suffering in silence.

We also talked about the role the music industry can play in the mental health community and how Alessia is using her celebrity and personal profile to let people know they are not alone in their struggles. Having the chance to get in-depth and personal about mental health with someone of Alessia's public stature was a significant experience the community responded to with sweeping favour.

Scan the QR code to watch the DLC interview with Alessia Cara

PARIS BERELC ON THE MENTAL HEALTH CHALLENGES OF FAME

Gen-Z actress Paris Berelc joined us in October of 2021 to talk about the impact of fame and the entertainment industry on mental health. Paris described her struggles with anxiety and mental health on-set and otherwise being in the public eye.

We talked about what the entertainment industry is doing well in terms of mental health resources and what it can improve on. Paris was kind enough to answer questions from the community about getting into acting and the entertainment industry when anxiety and depression are in the mix. Her experience was invaluable in that respect.

She was also very adamant about the need to speak up when we struggle. Her interview allowed us a deeper look at the mental health struggles that come along with living a very public life.

Scan the QR code to watch the DLC interview with Paris Berelc

BEYOND MY OWN EXPERIENCE – THE EVOLUTION OF THE DLC ANXIETY COMMUNITY

As of this writing, over fifty of these types of interviews are available on the DLC Anxiety platform on Instagram and on the *DLC Live* podcast. They represent a wide range of experiences, opinions, educational backgrounds, and areas of expertise when it comes to anxiety and overall mental health. The interview series includes actors, musicians, doctors, therapists, mental health advocates, and social media celebrities—all coming together to educate, inform, support, and empower our community. The DLC interview series has proven to be incredibly useful for so many members of the community. The feedback has been tremendously positive and encouraging. It continues to motivate me to do more every day.

Even before my first interview with Dax, the DLC platform was moving beyond just my experience. It was a natural progression already in progress, but this addition to the platform kicked that transformation into high gear. The depth and breadth of experience and information that these interviews brought to the platform firmly planted the community onto a wider, more diverse base. I could not be happier about that.

Everyone's personal experiences matter in the DLC community. Everyone is welcome to share. I'm proud of the engagement and the sharing we see on a daily basis.

We might not all be famous, but we all matter.

That said, relating directly to admired entertainers and respected teachers and helpers adds something special to the mix that can't easily be put into words. Allowing us to see that our guides are here for us and that our heroes are also human can make a difference at any given moment. When you feel hopeless and lost, knowing that there is hope and seeing that hope lived by someone who might otherwise seem beyond the struggle is invaluable.

So here we sit, younger and older, famous and not so famous, from all walks of life and all corners of the world gathered under an umbrella of sharing and support. In the DLC Anxiety community, you may be inspired by a school teacher from Cardiff, a world-renowned psychiatrist, or a multi-platinum-selling recording artist.

You just never know, and I am over the moon that it turned out this way—that my vision blew up beyond anything I could have hoped for.

CHAPTER 12

FINAL THOUGHTS AND INSPIRATION

We started this book in the middle of a panic attack, with all the scary symptoms and feelings that come with it.

You may have picked it up feeling isolated, with little to no motivation and no clear path out of anxiety and panic. You may have felt disconnected from the people around you and retreated from the things you used to love doing.

Throughout this journey, you've seen that the uncomfortable sensations and feelings that you can probably relate to are very real. You've seen that anxiety and panic did not harm me and cannot harm you. You've learnt that the panic and anxiety response is a natural response to danger. It is a normal, natural reaction to a threat, either perceived or real. In an anxiety disorder, this threat response is misfiring, trying so convincingly to tell us that we are in danger when we are not.

My experience has illustrated that often the first methods we try in the hope of fixing our anxiety and panic are what keep us glued to an anxiety disorder. You now know avoidance backfires, and remaining silent to try to hide your anxiety and carry your burdens alone can make the situation worse than it has to be. I've talked about how there is no 'cure' for anxiety and why trying to eliminate it completely from our lives is not realistic or possible.

We've even talked about how anxiety is not always the enemy. You're aware now that anxiety is a normal part of being alive and that it does serve a useful purpose in keeping us alert and safe when there is real true danger afoot. In this light, I've tried to help you manage your expectations for what recovery has in store for you. Hopefully, this will help you avoid the many quick fixes and outrageous cures marketed so heavily on the internet today.

There is no quick fix.
There is no miracle cure.
There is no such thing as a life with zero anxiety.
But there IS real and lasting recovery when
we point ourselves in the right direction.

I've shared my experience with loss, grief, and the power of strong emotions. It is my hope that you've seen how my failure to acknowledge them and my attempt to bottle them all up and sweep them under the rug started me down a bad path. I hope I have encouraged you not to repeat my mistake and to honour and express your emotions in life. I know in my heart that this is the healthier way.

In discussing building an anxiety toolkit, I am hopeful that you can now see that while there is no one-size-fits-all solution for an anxiety disorder, making the effort to find the tools that work for you, then bundling them all in a toolkit you can rely on when needed, is well worth it when it comes to your recovery. You may have to go through a trial-and-error process to build your toolkit, but even when we decide to discard a tool, we learn something from it, and it can help us along the road to recovery.

We've talked quite a bit about psychoeducation, too. Understanding it is the first bit of power that we can take hold of as we learn the hows and whys of our anxiety symptoms. Knowing what they mean and, more importantly, what they *don't* mean is invaluable in addressing our initial fear, getting us up on our feet, and pointing us in the direction of real recovery. Gaining a basic understanding of how our brains work and how our threat response fires is often the initial step out of a dark place.

Psychoeducation is often the first tool in every recovery toolkit and remains the tool we rely on most throughout our journey.

In examining the science behind what worked for me in my recovery and what may hopefully work for you too, I hope you can appreciate now that there is a world full of dedicated researchers and clinicians working hard to build a body of knowledge about anxiety, anxiety disorders, and mental health. We should take advantage of that and use it for our greatest benefit.

The importance of community in any recovery—including my own—can't be denied. The golden message of this book is that this is a journey that you do not need to go through alone. Please take this message as one to give you great comfort in your times of need. Our community shows us that for all people at all stages of recovery, there is light at the end of the road.

Our community has taught us that anxiety does not attack a special age, race, economic status, or level of notoriety.

Anyone can experience anxiety problems under any circumstances and at any time in their lives. In the DLC Anxiety community, we share in the stories of regular people like you and me, but we've also gained insight and experience from celebrities who have shared their mental health struggles and victories. Seeing what has worked for them in their recovery journeys and hearing their unique points of view about the impact of fame on mental health has been invaluable—it proves to us that even people who seem to have it all can still struggle. We don't know what we don't know about other people.

The privilege of learning from some of the world's leading mental health professionals and advocates has provided us with some of the leading methods, techniques, and strategies they use when addressing mental health issues like anxiety and depression.

In the end, I hope that this book has inspired you to take some steps towards recovery in whatever way works for you. Maybe you can follow my steps. They may resonate with you. They may work for you. You may have to take a detour here and there to find what fits best in your specific situation. You may have to do a bit of trial-and-error work and may stumble at times. You'll probably even make mistakes along the way (we all do!). But you can always pick yourself back up and keep going.

There is always hope. There is always a way out, no matter how long and dark the road may seem at times.

Every day in our community, we see not only struggles but victories. Some small. Some big. We can use these victories to inspire and encourage us during the toughest times and know that recovery is possible for all of us. It was possible for me, even though at times I could not see that. I'm just a regular guy who once had an anxiety disorder, but now I do not. I'm not special. I'm no smarter or stronger than you. If I can do it, I believe in my heart that you can too, one step at a time.

Speaking of which, maybe it's time to start putting one foot in front of the other. What if today was the day you started down the path to recovery? I know that the path may be a long, winding, unpredictable, and sometimes steeply pitched road, but I also know it is a walkable path. As you travel upon it, you will not be alone. Take each individual step, and never forget to celebrate your accomplishments, no matter how small they may feel. Each one counts, and they all add up to the life that you want so badly right now.

My most sincere wish for you is for a complete recovery and full life. One day, I hope that you will look back at your journey and know that every step you took was *greater than panic*. That the work you did was *greater than panic*. That the lessons you learnt were *greater than panic*. That your friends and family were *greater than panic*. That your community was *greater than panic*.

One day I hope you will see that *YOU* are *greater than panic*.

RESOURCES

If you would like to access the online resources listed below, scan this QR code to visit the DLC Anxiety website where all the links can be found in easily clickable form.

National Alliance on Mental Illness (NAMI)
@NAMI.org

Mental Health America (MHA)
@mhanational.org

National Institute for Mental Health (NIMH)
@NIMH.NIH.gov

Rethink Mental Health Incorporated
@RETHINKstigma.org

Boo2bullying
@boo2bullying.org

Anxiety and Depression Association of America
@ adaa.org

International OCD Foundation
@iocdf.org

Dr. Daniel Amen (psychiatrist)
@DanielAmenMD.com

Dr. Julie Smith (psychologist)
@DoctorJulieSmith.com

Dr. Radha (Doctor)
@DrRadha.co.uk

Cognitive behavioral therapy in anxiety disorders: current state of the evidence:
https://www.ncbi.nlm.nih.gov/pmc/articles/PMC3263389/

The effect of mindfulness meditation on sleep quality: a systematic review and meta-analysis of randomized controlled trials:
https://www.ncbi.nlm.nih.gov/pmc/articles/PMC6557693/

How Meditation Can Treat Insomnia:
https://www.sleepfoundation.org/insomnia/treatment/meditation

Maximizing Exposure Therapy: An Inhibitory Learning Approach:
https://www.ncbi.nlm.nih.gov/pmc/articles/PMC4114726/

Randomized Controlled Trial of Mindfulness Meditation for Generalized Anxiety Disorder: Effects on Anxiety and Stress Reactivity:
https://www.ncbi.nlm.nih.gov/pmc/articles/PMC3772979/

Headspace: Mindfulness and Meditation App With Free Resources

Durable Effects of Cognitive Restructuring on Conditioned Fear
https://www.ncbi.nlm.nih.gov/pmc/articles/PMC3971472/

Cognitive Behavioral Therapy for Anxiety and Related Disorders: A
Meta-Analysis of Randomized Placebo-Controlled Trials
https://www.ncbi.nlm.nih.gov/pmc/articles/PMC5992015/

Journaling For Mental Health:
https://www.urmc.rochester.edu/encyclopedia/content.aspx?ContentID
=4552&ContentTypeID=1

Why Don't Therapists Use Exposure? And How Psychological Flexibility
Can Help
https://drericmorris.com/2014/07/08/why-dont-therapists-use-
exposure-and-how-psychological-flexibility-can-help/

Why do clinicians exclude anxious clients from exposure therapy?:
https://pubmed.ncbi.nlm.nih.gov/24530499/

ABOUT THE AUTHOR

Dean had an interest in the mind from a young age, and went on to study psychology at university. He then pursued a career in sales.

Following the passing of his father, Dean developed an unexpected anxiety disorder and had to battle with it for two years, often experiencing several panic attacks a day. After overcoming the anxiety disorder, Dean wanted to dedicate his life to helping others speak freely about mental health and showing them that it was possible to recover from an anxiety disorder.

Dean furthered his education and gained qualifications in coaching and cognitive behavioural therapy for depression, anxiety and phobias.

Dean decided he wanted to go full-time helping others and this is when the DLC Anxiety community was born. Fast forward two and a half years and DLC Anxiety (Dean's like-minded community) has amassed an incredible 1.1 million followers. DLC Anxiety is a mental health community that is packed with educational resources and interviews with mental health professionals and celebrities around the globe.

DISCLAIMER

Greater Than Panic is not therapy nor should it be construed as a substitute for professional medical or mental health advice. The information is provided for educational and informational purposes and is not intended to diagnose or treat you in any way. Reading *Greater Than Panic* and interacting with the author in any way does not create a therapist/client or counsellor/client relationship. Please, always consult your medical and mental health providers for questions about your health and well-being.

Printed in Great Britain
by Amazon